BAPTIST
FOUNDATIONS
IN THE
SOUTH

BAPTIST FOUNDATIONS IN THE SOUTH

Tracing through the Separates the Influence of the Great Awakening, 1754-1787

William L. Lumpkin

PUBLISHERS
Eugene, Oregon

Wipf and Stock Publishers
199 W 8th Ave, Suite 3
Eugene, OR 97401

Baptist Foundations in the South
Tracing through the Separates the Influence of the Great Awakening, 1754-1787
By Lumpkin, William L.
ISBN: 1-59752-705-X
Publication date 5/22/2006
Previously published by Broadman Press, 1961

Preface

THE GREAT AWAKENING, an unprecedented movement of religious revival, appeared early in the eighteenth century in Great Britain, in Protestant Europe, and in America. In the New World its earliest manifestations were in the Middle Colonies among Reformed and Presbyterian congregations. Soon afterward, it appeared in New England in the established Congregational churches.

As the first general revival of religion in America, the Awakening profoundly affected the life of the colonies, introducing a new religious earnestness, purifying and elevating moral and ethical standards, and contributing markedly to the nonconformist character of American religion and idealism.

Some twenty years after the Awakening appeared in other regions of colonial America, the revival movement reached the South. It was promoted successively there by the Presbyterians, the Baptists. and the Methodists. The Baptist phase of the southern Awakening was more far-reaching in its consequences than either the Presbyterian or the Methodist phases.

No group heralded religious revival so enthusiastically or so extensively in the period 1755-75 and none benefited by it so generously as the Baptists. Borne upon a tide of exciting religious conquest and following a definite plan of regional expansion, they not only ministered to multitudes but also laid sure foundations for future denominational strength in the three decades after the middle of the eighteenth century.

It must be noted, however, that the Baptist awakening was not in any primary sense the concern or achievement of the "regular" Baptist groups already resident in the South prior to 1755. It was, rather, the work of a handful of rugged, single-minded, enthusiastic colonists from Connecticut who, for their "irregularity," were known as "Separate" Baptists. These settled at Sandy Creek in central North Carolina in 1755 and immediately introduced the phenomenon of revival to the southern frontier.

Shubal Stearns was the guiding genius behind the Separate Baptists. Although he lacked formal preparation for the ministry and by middle age had made no outstanding record of religious leadership in his native New England, he proved himself capable of inspiring and directing a religious movement of surprising proportions in the South the last sixteen years of his life. Unfortunately, he wrote little, and almost nothing of his writing has been preserved. He was essentially a man of vision, action, and administrative ability. His preaching, unexcelled in persuasive power, quickened the religious life of thousands and became the model for the preaching of a region and an era. The clouds of witnesses roused by his ministry were deliberate echoes of his living voice.

Efforts have been made to assess the total effect upon the South of the Great Awakening, but no thorough study of the southern revival from the standpoint of a single denomination has been undertaken. Certainly, the most important of the three phases of the Awakening in the South deserves special study.

Rarely has a denomination established itself in a region so rapidly as the Separate Baptists in the South. Without the favorable reputation claimed by the earlier Presbyterians or the efficient organization used later by the Methodists, the Separate Baptists securely planted themselves within twenty years following their arrival at Sandy Creek, North Carolina. Their story forms an important chapter in the record of American church history.

The accomplishments of the Separate Baptist movement are extremely remarkable since Baptists prior to 1755 were an insignificant and generally despised sect in America. Indeed, in England, also, where Baptist churches had begun to appear as early as the beginning of the seventeenth century, they continued to occupy the status of a reluctantly-tolerated, minor dissenting sect through the eighteenth century. Neither in England nor in

America did they have official support or a large popular following before 1750. Yet, they were destined in the providence of God to serve as chief instruments for planting the Christian faith along the southern frontier of early America.

The Baptists today are easily the largest Christian group in the southern portion of the United States. In no other region of the entire world are they so numerous and influential. Their prosperity is mainly due to environmental factors of culture and economy. Also, their priority in occupying the eighteenth-century southern frontier gave them a position of great advantage. It has long been accepted as axiomatic that those denominations which most closely followed America's frontier expansion were destined to be America's strongest denominations.

The triumph of free-church principles in the Revolutionary era, the homogeneity of southern people, and the rise of the common man and the economically depressed in the South are among the factors which have contributed to Baptist growth in the region. However, circumstances associated with Baptist beginnings in the South have been overlooked too long as a factor contributing to this growth. Study will reveal that the life and history of the Separate Baptists have continued to leave their mark upon the subsequent story of the denomination and the nation.

Contents

1. Separatism in Connecticut 1

2. Called Forth and Entering In 24

3. The Promised Land: Its Possession Begun 33

4. Brush Fires in All Directions 46

5. Are They Blood Brothers? 60

6. Persecution and Exodus 72

7. All Ablaze in Virginia 87

8. Persecution and Struggle for Freedom in Virginia 104

9. Claiming the Western Frontier 121

10. Post-Revolutionary Revival and Merger 133

11. Significance of the Movement 147

    Bibliography 163

Separatism in Connecticut

1

THE ACTUAL BEGINNINGS of the Great Awakening in New England extend back to 1734 and the leadership of Jonathan Edwards at Northampton, Massachusetts. From his small-town pastorate, Edwards launched a movement to rescue a state-church Congregationalism which was fast losing its hold upon the people.

Apparently, vital religion in the region had begun to deteriorate with the second generation of colonists. This decline was largely due to the fading of the early Congregationalist ideal of the church. The vigor of early Congregationalism had been a direct result of the first-generation fathers' conviction that "visible saints are the only true and meet matter, whereof a visible church should be gathered." In keeping with their covenant theology, they had regularly baptized their children as infants. They had not permitted them to become full church members, however, until the children had known an experience of grace and had agreed to submit themselves to the discipline of the church.

Many children attained maturity without being able to profess themselves regenerated saints, but they were accepted as church members. The right of these unconverted people to present their children for baptism became a matter of contention. After much discussion, the Massachusetts synod decided in 1662 that "their children are to be Baptized." The baptized children, however, were not given the right to vote, hold office in the church, or partake of the Lord's Supper. They were morally acceptable but without claim to sainthood. This arrangement was called the Halfway Covenant. Since acceptance of this practice was rapid and widespread, Congregationalism claimed a large class of inferior church members by 1720, baptized into the churches without conversion.

By 1720 the base of church membership was further broadened by Solomon Stoddard, of Northampton, when he advocated the admission of "Halfway" members to the Communion Table in the hope that their participation in the Supper might be the means whereby they would experience grace. "Stoddardianism" made church membership available to all people "not of scandalous life"; moral or even social acceptability became the qualifying test. The result was an almost complete disappearance of vital religion.

Then the relentless preaching by Jonathan Edwards of complete surrender to the will of God introduced the novel phenomenon of revival in Massachusetts. From Northampton the revival traveled down the Connecticut Valley into Connecticut in 1735. By June, 1736, some twenty parishes had been affected.[1] Interest in the movement prompted Edwards to write "A Faithful Narrative of the Surprising Work of God in the Conversion of Many Hundred Souls . . ." (1736).

The initial revival was of short duration, however, and did not touch the people of New England generally. Even in the Connecticut Valley many communities were not affected. Religious decline was not arrested in most areas. By 1737 the stirring had quite ceased, although numbers of pious ministers continued to pray for a quickening in their churches.

Prayers for a reawakening of the revival were answered in the arrival of George Whitefield, the world-famous English evangelist, at Newport in September, 1740. A fresh surge of revival enthusiasm may have been checked for several years by their feeling that it would not come until he should visit the area, but that it must come when he should arrive.[2] Whitefield's reputation had

---

[1] M. H. Mitchell, *The Great Awakening and Other Revivals in the Religious Life of Connecticut* (New Haven: Yale University Press, 1934), p. 9.

[2] F. W. Hoffman, *Revival Times in America* (Boston: W. A. Wilde Co., 1956), p. 54.

preceded his arrival from England in 1739, and the entire populace of the colonies had heard with a thrill about the multiplied successes of his preaching as he toured the Middle and the Southern Colonies in the months before he came to New England. Churches in New England eagerly expected his coming to bring a mighty visitation of grace. They were not disappointed.

Great crowds greeted Whitefield as soon as he landed. In Boston since churches could not contain the crowds seeking to hear him, he moved out of doors onto the Common. Throngs as large as fifteen thousand pressed upon him there. Whitefield records in his journal that "many wept exceedingly, and cried out under the Word, like persons that were hungering and thirsting after righteousness. The Spirit of the Lord was upon them all."[3] After about a month around Boston, Whitefield journeyed to Northampton in October to meet Jonathan Edwards. Revival fires immediately reappeared in that place. Edwards said that his congregation was "melted by every sermon."

But not for long would the relentless Whitefield tarry; in seventy-five consecutive days of 1740 he preached from place to place 175 times.[4] Leaving Northampton, he headed for Connecticut. There he preached, pausing for a few hours at each place, in Suffield, Westfield, Springfield, East Windsor,[5] Hartford, Weathersfield, and Middletown. Congregations grew as he proceeded.

Soon he reached New Haven, where the aged Governor Talcott welcomed him with tears of joy. The legislature of the colony adjourned in his honor; and the governor, the council, and members of the lower house of the Assembly came to hear him preach. Mr. Clap, rector of Yale College, entertained him and had him address the students. Whitefield warned them of the evils of an unconverted ministry.

After three days in New Haven, the preacher was on the march

---
[3] *Ibid.*
[4] A. H. Newman, *A History of the Baptist Churches in the United States* (New York: Charles Scribner's Sons, 1915), p. 242.
[5] Edwards accompanied him this far.

again. He paused to preach in Milford, Stratford, Fairfield, Newark, and Stamford in Connecticut before leaving New England for New York. All Connecticut was at his feet. As Williston Walker asserts, "Never in the history of New England was a preacher possessed of such popular influence or received with such unbounded admiration by the community at large."[6] In a brief six-weeks' period, the religious climate of New England was changed. "There are few instances in history of transformations of religious life so profound and so widespread during so short a period," Newman says.[7]

The revival continued with increasing fervor even after Whitefield left in October, 1740. The climax was yet to come, in the spring and the summer of 1741, and the highest enthusiasm remained through 1742. All New England saw an outburst of evangelistic activity, but no region was more strongly affected than Connecticut.

Whitefield's visit there was followed shortly by one from Gilbert Tennant, the fiery Presbyterian evangelist from New Jersey.

The churches experienced unprecedented growth. The two in North Stonington and Franklin received over one hundred converts in 1740; the former had received only sixty-five in the previous nine years. The church in Groton added eighty in a six months period in 1740, and the two churches in Lyme gained about two hundred and fifty new members in 1740-41.[8] The eastern part of the colony felt the Awakening much more than the western part. Great revivals broke out in Norwich, Preston, Stonington, Groton, New London, and Lyme in 1740.[9] Entire communities flocked to hear the gospel, and hundreds were converted in single localities.

---

[6] Williston Walker, *A History of the Congregational Churches in the United States* (New York: Christian Literature Co., 1894), p. 258. L. Tyerman, *The Life of the Rev. George Whitefield* (New York: Randolph & Co., 1877), I, 429-30.

[7] *Loc. cit.*

[8] Mitchell, *op. cit.*, p. 12.

[9] Frederic Denison, *Notes of the Baptists, and Their Principles, in Norwich* (Norwich, 1857), p. 12.

The Great Awakening emphasized individual conversion and the new birth. The conversion experience which men were taught to seek was both exciting and painful. Steps in the experience included an "awful apprehension" of one's sinfulness and depravity, submission of one's self to the sovereign will of God, dependence upon his grace and justice whatever the outcome, and great happiness and relief at the thought of having been elected eternally.[10]

Once the excited converts had broken through the reserve of sober Puritanism, they might well have been expected to give dramatic expression to their feelings. Such manifestations appeared under the preaching of both Edwards and Whitefield, and both men saw validity in them and at first took no steps to suppress them. They were regarded as marks of divine favor. However, some of the preachers and exhorters who followed Edwards and Whitefield, supposing that the approval of such manifestations by the greatest preachers of their acquaintance gave them license to exploit this form of excitement, encouraged extravagant emotional display. Hysterical "screechings, cryings out," shouting, barking, dancing, trances, and visions became common in some areas. These manifestations "assumed the character of an epidemic" toward the climax of awakening in 1740.

The most radical exponent of such emotionalism was James Davenport, of Southold, Long Island, great-grandson of the founder of New Haven and a close friend of Whitefield. He came to Stonington, Connecticut, in July, 1741. His first preaching there converted one hundred persons, but he soon created a scandal by his noisy and eccentric conduct. In New Haven he induced confusion and divided the church. In Boston near riots followed his preaching in June, 1742. Back in Connecticut in March, 1743, at New London he publicly burned his possessions, including jewels, clothes, and books. Both the Connecticut legislature and the General Court of Massachusetts adjudged him mentally unbalanced. His statement in 1744 retracting his

---

[10] Mitchell, *op. cit.*

excessive conduct neither encouraged men to forget nor discouraged some preachers from imitating his extravagances. Other revivalists continued to stress emotionalism. Excesses were nowhere more conspicuous than in eastern Connecticut.[11]

There can be no doubt that many earnest churchmen were prejudiced against the revival by the disorder and tactlessness of some preachers. Closely allied with this source of prejudice was another, an aggressive itinerant evangelism. Daniel Wadsworth reflected this concern when, in 1740, he said of Whitefield, "What to think of the man and his Itinerant preaching I scarcely know."[12] Whitefield was a full-time itinerant, and he raised up a small army of itinerants. Settled pastors temporarily left their parishes and went from place to place to assist other pastors in special services. Edwards often left Northampton for this purpose.

Other pastors who gave much time to itinerant evangelism included Jonathan Parsons, of Lyme; Benjamin Pomeroy, of Hebron; Eleazer Wheelock, of Lebanon; Joseph Bellamy, of Bethlem; and John Graham of Southbury. Their preaching also produced physical demonstrations among their audiences.[13] The traveling preachers generally fashioned their preaching after that of Whitefield, an informal and extemporaneous delivery on theological rather than simply moral themes.

Many enthusiastic lay evangelists also appeared, which seemed to many the height of disorder. But there was no stopping the assembling of the awakened folk as the Awakening early became a people's movement. These informal groups sent out preachers who were utterly without formal training for the ministry and who invaded parishes without invitation.

A third source of offence occasioned by the revival was the sharp criticism hurled by revivalists at the established ministry. Conservative groups, particularly in Connecticut, became alarmed. In this, too, the example of Whitefield was prominent. "Hypo-

---

[11] *Ibid.*, p. 15 Joseph Tracy, *The Great Awakening* (Boston: Tappan & Dennet, 1842), pp. 248-49.
[12] Mitchell, *op. cit.*, p. 11.
[13] Walker, *op. cit.*, p. 259.

crites" and "wolves in sheep's clothing" were epithets he hurled at the unconverted or antirevivalistic clergy, and he did not hesitate to go uninvited into their parishes. Preaching at Norwich in 1740, he "did not spare" the unconverted ministers, and in the same year he warned the Yale students against such ministers. He must have felt deep justification for his attacks upon unconverted preachers when the Connecticut General Consociation formally declared in 1740 that regularly chosen and ordained men were "lawful ministers of Christ, even if after all they should Really be Unconverted men."[14]

All of these offensive aspects of Whitefield's ministry were referred to in the "Testimony" of the faculty of Harvard College on December 28, 1744, "against the Rev. Mr. George Whitefield and his conduct." This document charged Whitefield with enthusiasm; with being "an uncharitable, censorious and slanderous man"; and condemned his extempore and "itinerant way of preaching."[15]

The mighty revival interest following Whitefield's 1740 visit drew many people together into informal societies which promised to become churches. Converts joining existing churches soon felt ill at ease at the coldness and hostility of the unawakened members. Whether remaining in the old churches or counting themselves members of separate societies, the new converts were dubbed "New Lights" by their critics because the awakened people emphasized the immediacy of the Holy Spirit's illumination and leadership in their personal lives. The conservatives of the old churches were then reckoned "Old Lights." The former favored Whitefield's type of evangelism and the idea of the regenerate church; the latter opposed revivalism and defended the state church order.

New England was thus speedily divided into two church parties. The Connecticut legislature was conscious of the magnitude of the problem as early as October, 1741, when it approved a

---
[14] Mitchell, op. cit., p. 14.
[15] Tracy, op. cit., pp. 247-50.

proposition of the ministers to have a general consociation for "the accommodation of divisions, settling peace, love, and charity, and promoting the true interest of vital religion."

The consociation which met at Guilford, November 24, 1741, declared against itinerant preachers and stated that no minister should preach in the parish of another without the incumbant's consent. This did not remedy the situation, however, and the General Court the following May forbade all itinerant preaching. The penalty for such preaching was loss of the right to collect one's legal salary and imprisonment. Itinerant lay preachers or strange ministers were to be silenced or expelled from the colony.[16]

By 1744 the informal societies of New Lights were assuming the status of churches in actual practice. Numbers of converted members were being forced out of the old churches by the anti-revivalist members. Then the name "Separates" was referred to those awakened Christians who felt that churches should include only regenerate members and those who separated from state churches on this conviction.

Those New Lights who stayed for a time in the old churches agitated for the reinstatement of the concept of the pure church, but since they composed minorities in most churches they failed. Most Congregationalists of the time had no ambition to return to the "sect ideal" as Edwards' Northampton church had done. It required people presenting themselves for membership to sign a confession of their faith, to testify to their personal experience of divine grace, and to submit themselves to a careful discipline. To many New Lights, separation from the old churches seemed practical if their vital faith and that of the church was to be saved. Prejudice against the Separates grew increasingly bitter in 1744-45, attaining a virulence far more intense than that aimed at such dissenting groups as Baptists and Quakers in New England.

The Separate movement originated in Connecticut, especially in the eastern part of the state. Early Separate congregations appeared at Canterbury, Mansfield, Plainsfield, and Norwich. They

---

[16] Walker, *op. cit.*, p. 262.

preferred to be known as "Strict Congregational" churches.[17] These were largely made up of prorevivalists who had tried to live and to work transformations within the old churches but who, in one way or another, had been forced out.

The Separates carried their pattern of organization and church life from Connecticut into Massachusetts. Rejecting the tradition and authority of extracongregational bodies, they appealed to the higher authority of revelation. Their ministers possessed no official power among themselves greater than that of other members. All "gifted" members were allowed to preach, whatever their educational qualifications. The Lord's Supper was reserved for converted believers, and the aid of the civil power in administering church discipline was refused.

A confused situation faced Whitefield when he returned to New England for a second visit in the autumn of 1744. Although his personal triumph equaled that of 1740, he found all of New England now sharply divided into parties favoring or opposing revivalism. One thing was certain—a formidable body of opposition to him and his methods had developed in his absence of four years. Not long after landing at York, Maine, he found few pulpits open to him. A barrage of declarations and testimonies was aimed at him. In 1743 the convention of ministers of Massachusetts Congregational churches had gone on record as opposing the revival, although a minority of over sixty prorevivalists in the convention had met later in special session and expressed their appreciation for the "late happy Revival of Religion."[18] The faculty of Harvard College now stood definitely against Whitefield. This was provoked, no doubt, by his earlier criticisms of the college.

As the evangelist made his way southward, the authorities of Connecticut feared the possible consequences of his second visit to the colony. The General Association of the Congregational

---
[17] *Ibid.*
[18] Jacob C. Meyer, *Church and State in Massachusetts from 1740 to 1833* (Cleveland: Western Reserve University Press, 1930), p. 24.

Churches of Connecticut passed a resolution in June, 1745, advising ministers not to admit Whitefield to their pulpits and citizens not to attend his meetings. Yale College also opposed him.

Nevertheless, the preacher made his way to eastern Connecticut; and, in spite of the authorities, great crowds struggled to hear him. At Norwich, he learned that the established church there had already split. Nine days before his arrival the pastor, Dr. Lord, had sent a letter to thirteen persons who had ceased to attend regular meetings and had set up a separate meeting in a home. The letter demanded that the dissidents appear before the church and explain their conduct. Among these Separates were Isaac Backus, afterward the famous Baptist "Apostle of Liberty," and his mother. The seceders, strengthened by Whitefield's visit, appeared before the church and stated their position. They were not dissuaded from their independent course, not even by threats and punishment.[19]

Whitefield was greeted with enthusiasm in Norwich and elsewhere in eastern Connecticut. The fires of Separate revivalism flared anew. The people, at least the Separates, are said to have "regarded him as sent of God, like a flame of fire, to purify the land."[20] In August, the evangelist left eastern Connecticut for Long Island and the South.

Two men were strongly moved by Whitefield during his 1745 tour through Connecticut; they were to become chief instruments in carrying the Great Awakening to the South. Shubal Stearns, of Tolland, was then a Congregationalist, twenty-nine years of age. Daniel Marshall, of Windsor, was an experienced deacon and of the same age. Although strangers to one another in 1745, their lives were soon to be bound together, with momentous consequences for the religious life of their time.

Religious conditions in Connecticut were, in many respects, different from those in other parts of New England. The Puritan

---

[19] Denison, *op. cit.*, pp. 17, 20.
[20] *Ibid.*, p. 6.

tradition continued in greater strength there than elsewhere. Church and state were very closely linked. All citizens were taxed for the support of religion. The uniqueness of the state's religious situation lay in the church organization and leadership. While Massachusetts Congregationalists late in the seventeenth century shied away from a close connectionalism among their churches, those in Connecticut moved in the opposite direction toward a presbyterianized Congregationalism. In 1708 the Saybrook Platform, which greatly increased the power of the clergy, was adopted by the latter.

The platform provided for county associations of ministers, which met frequently to deal with matters of common interest and which were authorized to license young ministers. Beyond these associations, regional bodies called consociations were called for. They were composed of both ministers and laymen, and they were designed to handle all kinds of ecclesiastical difficulties, after the fashion of a Presbyterian synod. Then, at the top of the structure was placed the general association of the state, made up of delegates from the county associations, which exercised a general superintendency over churches and ministers. The effect of this efficient style of organization was to increase ministerial influence in church affairs and to add solidarity to the system through uniting ministerial strength with that of the most prominent laymen of the community. The Saybrook Platform was ordained by the legislature of Connecticut. Under it the established ministry was exceptionally secure.

The rule of religious uniformity had been challenged first in Connecticut, as in Massachusetts, by the Baptists, then by the Anglicans and Quakers. Baptist preachers came over from Rhode Island as early as 1674. These gained some converts and baptized them in the towns of Groton and Waterford. Their incursions were strenuously opposed by the authorities, and they were forced to operate clandestinely.[21]

---
[21] Philip Evans, *History of Connecticut Baptist State Convention, 1823-1907* (Hartford: Smith-Tinsley Co., 1909), p. 5.

In 1704 a few Baptists in Groton petitioned the General Court for liberty to establish a church in that town under provisions of the British Act of Toleration. The court ignored the request, and the petitioners, taking silence for consent, organized their church in 1705. They called the gifted young Rhode Island preacher Valentine Wightman as their first pastor. A bare toleration, and that perhaps unofficial, was accorded these Baptists, and the state church was careful that their society should not multiply.[22]

Nevertheless, Baptists continued to make a few converts in small-town and rural areas, although they made almost no headway in the larger towns. A second church supposedly was organized in Waterford about 1710.[23] The legislature, alarmed at Baptist growth, passed a statute in 1723 forbidding private meetings and baptisms except by a regular minister of a licensed congregation. In 1729, however, Baptists and Quakers were guaranteed the same legal privileges as the Anglicans.[24]

Other Baptist churches appeared in New London in 1726, Wallingford in 1735, and Farmington in 1739.[25] All of these probably were General (Arminian) Baptists. Arminian theological views had challenged and replaced the dominant Calvinism, which had characterized the earliest Baptist churches in that region except in about six New England churches. These revised views had not produced an aggressive evangelism or church life.

All dissenters were taxed for the support of the established religion except when they could "certificate off" and pay the tax to their own churches. This "exemption," allowable after 1729, was conditional upon the dissenters' attending their own churches regularly and living within five miles of their places of meeting. Persons with no church membership were taxed for the support of the Congregational ministry. The effort to silence exhorters

---

[22] *Ibid.*, p. 6.
[23] Denison, *op. cit.*, p. 10. The 1710 church probably did not live beyond a few years.
[24] Richard J. Purcell, *Connecticut in Transition, 1775-1818* (Washington: American Historical Association, 1918), pp. 66-67.
[25] Denison, *op. cit.*

and unlicensed preachers of the Great Awakening in 1742 led to temporary repeal of the Connecticut toleration acts. This development threatened to destroy the three or four Baptist societies then existing in Connecticut.[26]

In the developing religious conflict after 1740, the New Lights separated farther from the churches of the old order. The great bone of contention was the desire of the New Lights to limit church membership to the regenerate. Their doctrine was that "it is the will of God to have a pure church upon the earth, in this sense, that all the converted should be separated from the unconverted." The response of the antirevivalists was, in the words of the Wyndham County ministers, "to separate all true believers from those who are only nominally, but yet professedly so, and by their outward works and doctrines not proved to be otherwise, is to set up two visible kingdoms of Christ in the world, and to take one of these visible kingdoms out of another." These ministers further argued that since it was impossible to know who was converted and who was not, the church was obliged to accept any who offered themselves for membership. The New Lights held that saints could recognize the truly converted and that only such should be admitted to the churches.[27]

This division within Congregationalism may have extended as far back as the adoption of the Saybrook Platform, and the Whitefield revival only served to bring it into focus. Increase Mather's prophecy of 1705 was coming to pass: "If the begun apostasy should proceed as fast the next thirty years as it has done these last, surely it will come to pass in New England (except the Gospel itself depart with the order of it) that the most conscientious people therein will think themselves concerned to gather churches out of churches."[28] The separation of the Separates might have been forgiven; but when they adopted closed communion in their societies and refused to accept letters of dismissal from churches

---

[26] Newman, *op. cit.*, p. 231.
[27] Tracy, *op. cit.*, p. 318.
[28] Newman, *op. cit.*, p. 241.

of the standing order and to recognize them as true churches of Christ, bitter warfare followed. Solomon Paine's tract on the difference between the church of Christ and the church established by Connecticut laws was typical. The separation was underway!

Among the earliest Separate societies to become churches were those at Canterbury, Mansfield, Plainfield, Norwich, New London, Preston, Lyme, Middletown, and Suffield. They were made up chiefly of people of below-average circumstances. Over thirty Separate congregations were formed in the state, but fully half of them fell prey to persecution and died within twenty years.[29] Backus[30] mentions the ordination of thirty-one men as pastors of Separate churches from September, 1746 to May, 1751.

The established church felt justified in compelling the Separates to return to the fold of the old churches. As early as 1741 the civil government used repressive measures, for its aid had been sought to prevent and suppress religious disorders.

At first this persecution added fuel to the fire of New Light enthusiasm. Revivalistic ministers were shut out of meeting houses;[31] members were removed from civil office and, when they refused to pay taxes for the support of the regular ministry, imprisoned. At least until 1755 their petitions for relief were rejected. Imprisoned folk were called martyrs, and they acted the part, glorying in their sufferings and preaching the gospel of peace to all who would listen. Ultimately, however, the relentless pressure of the law, together with internal disharmony, forced many of the Separates to conform to the state churches.

Anti-New Light legislation in Connecticut may be summed up under three heads. First, laws were passed against unauthorized preaching (itineracy) and formation of churches. The Separates

---

[29] Albert G. Palmer, *A Discourse Delivered at the 100th Anniversary of the First Baptist Church in North Stonington, September 20, 1843* (Boston: Gould, Kendall, & Lincoln, 1844), p. 10.

[30] Isaac Backus, *A History of New England with Particular Reference to the Denomination of Christians Called Baptists* (Providence, 1784), II, 175.

[31] About half the ministers of Connecticut become New Lights, far more than in other parts of New England.

considered these as attempts to rob them of their essential liberties and to thwart the work of the Holy Spirit. Second, members of Separate societies and churches were taxed to support the standing churches and imprisoned when they refused to pay. Church taxes were levied, of course, by members in good standing in the local Congregational church. It was a matter of self-interest to distribute the tax load among as many people as possible. Separates were willing to be called dissenters, if need be; but the authorities were not willing to give them the privileges accorded Baptists, Quakers, and Anglicans. These privileges, as has been noted, were suspended in 1742.

Third, unauthorized schools and colleges were prohibited, and only university graduates were eligible for ministerial standing before the law. Thus, the example of the mother country was followed in the attempt to cut off dissenting leadership through denying educational opportunity. Here clerical hands took full control of the educational system. Children of Separates were not permitted to attend the established schools, and Separate schools were denied without a special license from the General Assembly. Acquiring a license was all but impossible.[32]

The logic of events pushed the Separates more and more in the direction of the Baptists, with whom there appears to have been a sympathy from the first appearance of the Separates. As long as the Toleration Act was operative, Separate groups might have claimed privileges accorded dissenters by changing their name to Baptist; but this was not long possible. Apparently, few groups took the Baptist name to escape the tax levies.

Affinity between Baptists and Separates rested upon a rather broad basis of agreement. Both advocated a regenerate church membership and rejected the Halfway Covenant theory, and both hated governmental interference with the churches. Both were wary of strong interchurch control and favored democratic ideals. The Separates liked the way the Baptists practiced

---

[32] E. S. Gaustad, *The Great Awakening in New England* (New York: Harper & Bros., 1957), p. 108.

democracy in their churches. In the regular Congregational churches, as they well knew, people sat according to their social position. If a family lost its wealth, it moved to a back seat. Not so, the Baptists. Both groups had an intense interest in religious liberty and represented the discontented element in society. Their views of the ministry and of ordination were almost identical, and, finally, they bore a similar relationship to the same opponents.

It is true that the Great Awakening at first did not appeal to the Baptists of New England generally. They were not inclined to follow the lead of pedobaptists, and they would not commit themselves easily to a movement springing up in the state church. The Calvinistic and enthusiastic character of the movement also bothered some. Nevertheless, a few Baptist churches joined the revival work with great success.

The Second Church of Newport, a Calvinistic church led by John Comer, was one of them. Forty-eight converts were baptized into its fellowship between March and August, 1741.[33] While the First Church of Boston, under its Arminian pastor Jeremiah Condy rejected the revival, a revivalistic group of members withdrew to form a prosperous Second Church in 1743. Nearer Connecticut, the old Welsh-background Calvinistic churches of Swansea and Rehoboth, Massachusetts, at first aloof soon came alive with revival interest. It was not like Welshmen long to ignore a revival. An occasional General Baptist like Valentine Wightman, of Groton, favored the Awakening, but it was the Calvinistic Baptists who benefited most.

Separate preachers were the instruments which stirred several of the old Baptist churches. Isaac Backus records that "several lively preachers were received among the old Baptists in Narragansett, who had much success there."[34]

Conversely, Baptist elders began to cross the Connecticut line

---

[33] Edwin S. Gaustad, "Baptists and the Great Awakening," *The Chronicle*, XV (1952), 42.

[34] Isaac Backus, *An Abridgement of the Church History of New England from 1620 to 1804* (Boston, 1804), p. 142.

from their homes in Rhode Island and Massachusetts, preaching to Separate groups requiring a ministry and baptizing some members of their churches. They were not slow to point out a position which some Separates were already beginning to take—that the surest safeguard of the pure or regenerate church concept was the practice of believers' baptism. This alone would keep the church distinct from the world. Infant baptism looked forward hopefully to a divine election, while believers' baptism testified to a salvation already secured.

Separate Congregationalists did not rush to leave their churches, even after they adopted antipedobaptist views. They continued in the fellowship of their Separate churches. This conformed with the ecumenical teachings of Whitefield and the Great Awakening.

Although many Separates were loath to give up infant baptism, more and more of them were persuaded to do so after 1749. It appeared for a while, says Backus, that all of the Separate churches would become Baptist. Then, when the new sentiment threatened to prevail over the old, sharp contests arose within many congregations between pedobaptists and antipedobaptists. Churches of the standing order encouraged the raising of a "fierce opposition" to "rebaptizing," and some Separates retracted what was termed their "very wicked act."[35] As early as 1741, Mr. Humphreys, of Derby, "had preached to a Baptist society and on that account was soon after deprived of a seat" in the Guilford Association. The next year, Philemon Robbins, minister in Branford, preached by invitation to the Baptist church in Wallingford. The New Haven Consociation tried him several times until 1745, when Robbins was made to "confess that he broke the law of God in preaching to the Baptists against their consent."[36]

The antipedobaptists, having derived their concept of church order from the Scriptures, would not recognize infant affusion as valid baptism. The pedobaptists wanted their fellows to recognize their own baptisms (received in infancy) at least.

---
[35] *Ibid.*, p. 192.
[36] Denison, *op. cit.*, p. 16.

Separate churches called councils, and a general meeting was held at Exeter in May, 1753.[37] Solomon Paine, of Canterbury, made a further attempt to arrange a compromise at Stonington in 1754. A three-day discussion involved forty churches: twenty-four in Connecticut, eight in Massachusetts, seven in Rhode Island, and one on Long Island. At the conclusion, the antipedobaptists still held that the pedobaptists were yet unbaptized, and the pedobaptists contended that rebaptism was a sacrilege.

The alliance of the two groups within Separatism was practically at an end, and the Baptist members left to form new churches or to join existing ones.[38] The communing of "real saints" and the sharing of the New Light enthusiasm had failed to unite them in the Separate churches. Baptist members shunned sitting at the Lord's Supper with those only sprinkled in infancy; they could not regard these friends as baptized Christians.

Perhaps the first large growth of Baptists occurred at Sturbridge, Massachusetts, in June, 1749; over sixty members were baptized, including all of the Separate church's officers. The elder Ebenezer Moulton preached and baptized others in Bridgewater and Raynham by the following September.[39] Apparently, not many Separate churches in Connecticut became Baptist churches entirely, but most had some antipedobaptist members who withdrew to join Baptist churches. These seceders often took their ministers with them. Of thirty-one ordained pastors of Separate churches in the period 1746-51, five were Baptists before they were ordained and eight became Baptists soon afterward.[40] Prominent Separate elders who submitted to baptism as believers included Ebenezer Mack, of Lyme; Joseph Hastings, of Suffield; Meacham, of Enfield; Marshall, of Somers; Matthew Smith; Elihue Marsh; Isaac Backus; William Carpenter; John Blunt; Samuel Hovey; and Shubal Stearns.[41]

---

[37] Backus, *Abridgement*, p. 192.
[38] Gaustad, "Baptists and Great Awakening," p. 45.
[39] Backus, *Abridgement*, p. 191.
[40] Newman, *op. cit.*, p. 245.
[41] Backus, *History of the Baptist*, p. 204.

The spiritual pilgrimage of Isaac Backus can be traced in more detail than that of almost any other New Light Baptist leader. Although he spent much of his ministry in Massachusetts, he was a native of Norwich, Connecticut; and his case well illustrates how New Light Congregationalists became Baptists.

Backus was converted to experimental religion in 1741 or 1742, early in the Awakening, and he joined the Congregational church for two years. He was soon disappointed in the pastor, Dr. Lord, who favored the "Saybrook scheme." The church had rejected it shortly before the pastor was settled. Moreover, the pastor looked upon the Supper as a "converting ordinance," after the manner of the Stoddardians. Most distressing of all to Backus, the pastor secured power from the church to admit new members "by a major vote, without giving the church so much as a written relation of any inward change."[42]

With twelve other members, Backus helped organize a Separate meeting in the home of Hugh Caulkins late in 1744 or early in 1745. Although these Sunday gatherings were held unlawfully, they grew rapidly. Also, the freedom with which laymen preached and exhorted in them created a public scandal. The parent church called them to account, and the dissenters suffered imprisonment. In 1746 Backus began his ministry of preaching. A congregation not formally a church called him as minister in December, 1747; it became the Titicut Church the next year.

The question of baptism was raised among his people in August, 1749, and three weeks of debate followed. The pastor decided in favor of believers' baptism after independent study, but not before ten of his members had been baptized by Baptist Elder Moulton in September, 1749. His own baptism waited awhile, however, when he learned of a libertine group in nearby Easton and Norton who baptized themselves and were said to practice community of wives. "Was this brand of lawlessness somehow associated with adult baptism?," he asked himself. Back to the Scriptures he went. His baptism followed on August 22, 1751.

---

[42] Backus, *Ibid.*, p. 206.

For a while Backus stayed with his mixed church, but controversy continued. There was no communion in the Supper from September, 1754 to the end of 1755. Finally, Backus led the Baptists in withdrawing to form the Middleborough Baptist Church in January, 1756.[43]

The religious interest in New England died out almost as fast as it had appeared. There were, for example, no conversions in Jonathan Edwards' church from 1744 through 1748. A sharp reaction arose against emotional and denunciatory preaching. Controversy claimed the attention of many, politics of others. A revival which had seen the conversion of perhaps forty thousand souls in New England was over.[44]

The Separate churches which remained Separate either died or slowly found their way back into fellowship with the Congregational churches of the older order. But long after the revival fires had burned low, the Baptists continued to profit from the movement. One after another, groups and churches of Separates found their way into the Baptist communion. They were, quietly but warmly, received by the now awakened Baptist churches. An unprecedented growth of this denomination followed. In 1740 not more than six of their Calvinistic churches are known to have existed in New England; by the end of the century there were at least 325 Baptist churches there, most of them Calvinistic.[45]

After Whitefield observed so many Separates becoming Baptists, he is reported to have said, "My chickens have turned to ducks." Sweet says that in the Awakening period proper, Baptist churches grew in numbers from six to thirty in Massachusetts, from four to twelve in Connecticut, from eleven to thirty-six in Rhode Island; and other churches were established in New Hampshire, Vermont, and Maine.[46]

This, then, was the religious and social background of Shubal

---

[43] *Ibid.*, pp. 207 ff.
[44] Denison, *op. cit.*, p. 40.
[45] Gaustad, "Baptists and Great Awakening," p. 43.
[46] W. W. Sweet, *The Story of Religion in America* (New York: Harper & Bros., 1950), pp. 149-50.

Stearns and Daniel Marshall, who brought the revival to the South and laid the foundations for the Baptist denomination in that region. Shubal Stearns was born in Boston, January 28, 1706, the son of Shubal and Rebecca Larriford Stearns. After he moved to Connecticut with his parents in his youth, he joined the Congregational church in Tolland, but he was converted to New Light views by Whitefield during his 1745 tour of Connecticut. Stearns met separately with the New Lights of the church in the same year, ministered to the awakened people, and led them to become a Separate church. In spite of many hinderances, his church steadily grew in strength until the pedobaptist-antipedobaptist controversy agitated it in 1751.

Since Wait Palmer, the New Light pastor of the Baptist church in North Stonington since 1743, itinerated much in the Tolland area, he may have been the first to call Stearns' attention to the baptism question. After Stearns made a thorough study of the Scriptures, he declared himself a Baptist. He was shortly baptized by Palmer at Tolland early in 1751.

The eloquence of Stearns persuaded many members of his Separate church to withdraw also and form a Baptist church in Tolland. With it, no doubt, were fused the fruits from the labors of Palmer and other Baptist preachers in that area. Stearns was ordained as pastor of the church on May 20, 1751, by Palmer and Joshua Morse, a Whitefield convert who only three days before had been ordained as pastor of the Baptist church in Monville, Connecticut.[47] Stearns served about three years.

Meanwhile, an excellent colaborer was being raised up in nearby Windsor. His experience concincided at many points with that of Stearns. Born in 1706 in Windsor and reared in a pious home, Daniel Marshall had a profound conversion experience in 1726. As a young man he was elected deacon in the First Congregational Church of Windsor,[48] an office he kept for about

---

[47] William Cathcart, *The Baptist Encyclopedia*, II, 181-82.
[48] J. D. Mosteller, *A History of Kiokee Baptist Church* (Ann Arbor: Edwards Bros., 1952), pp. 48-51.

twenty years. During that period he became a prosperous farmer, and on November 11, 1742, he married Hannah Drake. A son Daniel was born, but the mother died soon after.

Marshall married again on June 23, 1747; his second wife was Martha Stearns, of Tolland, Connecticut. Martha was a sister of the Separate preacher Shubal Stearns and a woman of stalwart character.

Marshall may have favored the Separate position as early as 1744. H. R. Stiles has produced evidence that Daniel Marshall made himself "odious to the othodox church in Windsor by preaching the Baptist doctrines" about that time.[49] These doctrines may have been nothing more than thoroughly democratic views of church polity or, possibly, opposition to infant baptism. He may have refused to have his son christened. The father himself had not yet been baptized.

After he had served as deacon for twenty years, the church found an opportunity to retaliate when Marshall's wife died. As the people assembled "to witness the funeral ceremony the pastor of the church refused to perform the usual service, upon which the people dispersed leaving the reverend widower to bury his deceased spouse himself."[50] This cruelty would have made Marshall a confirmed Separate at least, marking his final break with the old church.

Like Stearns, Marshall was deeply affected by George Whitefield during his 1745 tour. He may have heard the evangelist several times. This was about three years before Marshall married Martha Stearns.

A Separate meeting existed in Windsor as early as 1747. It may well be that Marshall had already offended his former associates by 1744 through acting as leader of the people disposed to Separatism. It is even possible, as Mosteller[51] suggests, that

---

[49] H. R. Stiles, *The History and Genealogies of Ancient Windsor, Connecticut, 1635-1891*, as quoted in James D. Mosteller, "The Separate Baptists in the South," *The Chronicle*, XVII (1954), 145.

[50] *Ibid.*, p. 145.

[51] Mosteller, *History of Kiokee Church*, p. 54.

Marshall was by conviction a Baptist and leader of the Baptist group in Windsor by 1750. He was certainly a Separate by 1747, and his marriage to the sister of Shubal Stearns may have helped to hurry him along the road to becoming a Baptist.

The Baptist meeting arose in Windsor by 1750 near Marshall's home on Poquonock Avenue. Moreover, it is recorded of Marshall's sister Eunice that, at an unnamed date, she "took upon herself to exhort and preach Baptist doctrines; was ordered to desist, but not obeying, was (although pregnant at the time), thrown into jail."[52]

Occasionally, groups which were Baptist by principles found it necessary to proceed without believers' baptism, until a Baptist minister should come along to administer the ordinance. Marshall may have presided over such a group.

Both Stearns and Marshall had become radical Separates by 1751. They were to be found leading small dissenting groups and living in a hostile atmosphere. They had willingly faced criticism and even social ostracism for their convictions, and they stood ready to obey any summons from the Lord. They had counted the cost of discipleship and had thought it their reasonable service.

---

[52] *Ibid.*

2

Called Forth and Entering In

IN THE HISTORY of Christian enthusiasm few groups have taken firmer hold on the doctrine of the immediate teaching of the Holy Spirit than the Separates of Connecticut. After Whitefield had assured them that knowledge of salvation comes through the heart, not the mind, they felt that all revelations of the divine will and purpose should be apprehended in the same way. The new birth meant participation in God's nature and illumination by the indwelling Spirit. The law-within took precedence over every human rule or convention in governing daily life.

With relentless intensity a twofold conviction was borne in upon the hearts of the Separates around 1750—the urgency of the missionary task and the readiness of men to accept the truth if only they could hear it. The Spirit seemed to be saying that time was short; if men were going to hear the gospel at all, they must hear it at once. Since all kinds of men were salvable, as many as possible must be given the opportunity to be saved. A frantic urgency filled the missionary enterprise.

Love for others, said Whitefield, stands alongside aversion to sin, a spirit of supplication, and a spirit of conquest over the world as a mark of having received the Holy Spirit.[1] Even the most unloved of men are loved by God. Thus, the savage Indian, a true representative of the grimness of the human situation, was an object of God's grace. As Whitefield spoke and taught and

---

[1] Stuart C. Henry, *George Whitefield, Wayfaring Witness* (Nashville: Abingdon Press, 1957), p. 124.

the people pondered and prayed, there arose a powerful impulse to evangelize the Indians of the frontier.

Daniel Marshall was among those who felt that the day of the Lord was fast approaching and that its coming might be hastened by his going forth to witness to men who had not heard the gospel. The voice of God was prompting him, a successful farmer and man of property, to devote his life to a ministry among the Indians.

Marshall did not act impulsively; he deliberately counted the cost of devoting himself to full-time Christian service. It was not easy to leave the comforts of home for the hardships of the wilderness. But when the voice of God called, he could not afford to ignore it. Some of Marshall's neighbors, under the powerful spiritual compulsion, hastily sold or gave away their possessions and headed for the nearest frontier in 1745 and 1746. But Marshall was not carried away by the excitement, for he did not start for New York until 1751 or 1752, over five years after he had heard Whitefield preach in 1745. It is probable that he did not dispose of his property in Windsor before leaving there.[2]

Already past his forty-fifth birthday, Marshall set out with his wife and three children for the forests of east-central New York.[3] One other couple also may have accompanied him.

Pushing northwestward, they crossed the Hudson and entered the territory of the Mohawk tribe in the region of the headwaters of the eastern branch of the Susquehanna River. The Mohawks were the easternmost tribe of the great Iroquois confederation called the Five Nations. This federal body held a dominant position among the Indian tribes of northeastern North America and represented the noblest governmental organization among aboriginal people of North America north of Mexico. The Five Nations, numbering some ten thousand souls in all, were already

---

[2] Mosteller, *op. cit.*, p. 55.
[3] His son Abraham wrote that his father had gone to the Indians "without the least prospect of a temporal reward." David Benedict, *General History of the Baptist Denomination in America and Other Parts of the World* (New York: Sheldon, Blakeman & Co., 1856), II, 351.

allied with the English against the French in the struggle for possession of North America. Thus, the Mohawks could be expected to treat English-speaking missionaries with kindness.

The Marshalls must have been received cordially. They were permitted to settle in a town called Onnaquaggy,[4] where Marshall's burning zeal found expression in missionary labors. The confidence of the Indians soon was won, and a new religious seriousness appeared in the village. A few of the Mohawks gave evidence of having received the gospel with power, but the great spiritual harvest of which Marshall had dreamed was not to be realized. After eighteen months of labor the mission had to be terminated.

Marshall had arrived among the Mohawks as the struggle between the English and the French in America was reaching a critical stage. The French were building fortifications and lining up Indian allies after 1750 throughout the Ohio country. The English were in danger of losing Indian allies because they were slow to erect forts and prepare for defense. By the end of 1753 French intrigue had succeeded in dividing the Five Nations.[5] The Mohawks, Oneidas, and Tuscaroras remained loyal to the British, while the Onondagas, Cayugas, and Senecas went over to the Delawares, the Shawanees, and other tribes allied with the French. The French induced these new recruits to persuade the Mohawks and others to side with the French. In this stratagem the allies of the French were markedly successful. The Mohawks were soon divided village against village. There were frequent clashes, and the danger of tribal warfare hung in the air.[6]

When strife among the Indians disrupted his work and threatened his family, Daniel Marshall left Onnaquaggy and moved

---

[4] The exact location of Onnaquaggy is uncertain. The name is not listed among known Mohawk towns by J. R. Swanton in *The Indian Tribes of North America,* Bulletin CXLV of the Smithsonian Institution of American Ethnology, Washington, 1952.

[5] Often called Six Nations by the addition of the Tuscaroras.

[6] Stewart Pearce, *Annals of Luzerne County* (Philadelphia: J. B. Lippincott & Co., 1960), pp. 34-35.

southward to Connogogig in Pennsylvania. Settling among European people, he is reported to have found it more difficult "to benefit scribes and pharasees than Publicans and sinners,"[7] and so he was on the move again after a short stay. Continuing southward, he arrived at Opekon (near Winchester), Virginia, some time in 1754.

At Opekon, Marshall must have been surprised to find a Baptist church. Named Mill Creek, or Opekon, this church dated from 1752[8] and was in fellowship with the Philadelphia Association. One of the two fully organized Particular (or Calvinistic) Baptist churches in Virginia, it had as its pastor Samuel Heaton.

Marshall and his wife were baptized by the Mill Creek pastor in 1754. It is possible that they were Baptist in sentiment before they reached Opekon and that they had not submitted to baptism earlier because no Baptist preacher had been available to administer it. Against this view is the testimony of Abraham Marshall, son of Daniel, that their baptisms took place "as the result of a close, impartial examination" of the faith and order of the Mill Creek Church. Daniel was forty-eight years old at that time. Joseph Breed and his wife, who may have accompanied the Marshalls to New York and thence to Virginia, also were baptized by Heaton.

Marshall's ability was recognized at Mill Creek at the time of his baptism, and he was soon licensed by the church "to the unrestrained exercise of his gifts."[9] Preaching as opportunity came, Marshall found a warm response in the community. In fact, Semple says, his preaching engendered such excitement that some of the "more cold-hearted" church members were shocked. Some even complained to the Philadelphia Association of what appeared to be disorder.

---

[7] J. B. Taylor, *Virginia Baptist Ministers* (Philadelphia: J. B. Lippincott & Co., 1859), I, 19.
[8] A General Baptist church had preceded it on Mill Creek.
[9] R. B. Semple, *A History of the Rise and Progress of the Baptists of Virginia,* revised and extended by G. W. Beale (Richmond: Pitt & Dickinson, 1894), p. 370.

The Association sent Benjamin Miller to investigate the report. To the evident disappointment of the "cold hearted," Miller could find nothing disorderly. Instead, he was delighted with what he saw and joined heartily in the revival services. In his report to the Association he stated that such warm-hearted Christians as he found in the Mill Creek church were worth more than gold. The revival continued in the fortunate church.[10]

Meanwhile, Shubal Stearns, pastor of the Baptist Church at Tolland, Connecticut, and brother-in-law of Marshall, felt that God had a great work for him somewhere on the western frontier. His missionary zeal stirred mightily, but he was uncertain where the divine appointment might take him. Probably, he had received communications from Marshall in Virginia, but these had not assured him that he was to fulfil his ministry in that area.

Nevertheless, Stearns hastened to order his affairs and those of his church, and he encouraged some of his church to consider accompanying their pastor westward. Five couples,[11] all or nearly all of them his kinfolk, decided to move with Stearns and his wife. These were Peter Stearns, Ebenezer Stearns, Shubal Stearns, Jr., Enos Stinson, Jonathan Polk, and their wives.

The church in Tolland was not to be left destitute of leadership. Noah Alden, who had been baptized only in July, 1754, but who could preach, was selected as the new minister of the congregation.

The party of migrants probably left Tolland in August, 1754, and made its way to New York, then to Philadelphia. Their possessions were drawn by cart. Continuing southward, the people would have turned to the west near Baltimore and proceeded up the Potomac Valley. They must have reached their destination in northern Virginia before cold weather.

After surveying the country with Daniel Marshall, who had greeted them and joined their company, they found a likely site for a settlement on Cacapon Creek, Hampshire County, Virginia. Homes were constructed hastily and other necessities of the

---
[10] *Ibid.*, p. 289.
[11] Six if Joseph Breed and his wife were in the party.

families met. Meanwhile the gospel had to be preached, and Stearns gave himself to the task. The area was sparsely settled, but Stearns soon felt that many more people should be attending his preaching services, which were held in homes and out-of-doors. He was further distressed at some members of neighboring Baptist churches who showed a very unco-operative spirit. These neighboring churches (later called "Regular" Baptist churches) upheld dignity and orderliness in worship; they were not used to the noisy and emotional preaching of the Separates. Also, doctrines which they occasionally heard from the Separate preachers may have suggested Arminianism to them, and the prominent place occupied by women in some Separate meetings hinted at disorder. If Mrs. Marshall were already exhorting as she did later in North Carolina, this would have been considered highly irregular in northern Virginia, regardless of her ability.

Under these conditions, Stearns questioned whether he had settled in the place of the Lord's appointment. Furthermore, the restlessness of the Indian tribes around his frontier settlement created a sense of insecurity. With the defeat of the British General Braddock in 1755, the Indians broke into open hostility, and the unprotected people then at Cacapon and Mill Creek were forced to move eastward across the Blue Ridge.

Stearns and his company, however, did not wait until they had to face the Indians. On June 13, 1755, Stearns received a letter from some New England friends who had gone to North Carolina; they explained the spiritual destitution and the need of a ministry there. The letter itself is not extant, but its contents are indicated in a letter which Stearns wrote to Connecticut from southern Virginia. In his letter the preacher said that the people in Carolina reported "that the work of God was great in preaching to an ignorant people, who had little or no preaching for a hundred miles, and no established meeting. But now the people were so eager to hear, that they would come forty miles each way, when they could have opportunity to hear a sermon."[12]

---

[12] Backus, *Abridgement*, p. 227.

The Stearns party left northern Virginia in the summer of 1755 and traveled down the Shenandoah Valley. At some point in the lower Valley, perhaps in Rockbridge or Roanoke counties, they crossed the Blue Ridge through a gap and entered the piedmont county of Pittsylvania. After they had crossed the interprovincial border, a journey of two hundred miles, they rested at Sandy Creek, Guilford (now Randolph) County, in central North Carolina.

The Sandy Creek area may have been suggested to Stearns by friends who had preceded him in North Carolina. Choice of the exact site at Sandy Creek may have been providential. Coming upon a juncture of forest trails in the midst of a great unoccupied area the settlers from New England quickly decided that they had seen no spot so promising. Was anyone on hand to greet them at the wilderness site? Where were their friends who had challenged them to come south? Evidently they did not reside at Sandy Creek. At any rate, none of them appears as a charter member of the church which was organized there.

Shubal Stearns must have observed the lay of the land and decided that this spot suited his intentions. He was not coming south for economic reasons, but to preach the gospel. He wanted a strategic center from which he could itinerate to a growing and spiritually destitute population. The wisdom of his choice of Sandy Creek was soon evident.

Although the people were weary and footsore, they set about once again to building houses and procuring food before the coming of cold weather. Also, a meeting house had to be erected; it was to be the center of the community. "As soon as they arrived," records Semple, "they built them a meeting house."[13] Just as quickly they formed themselves into a church of sixteen members. In addition to the eleven persons who accompanied Stearns to Virginia, there were, of course, Daniel Marshall and Joseph Breed and their wives who had joined the party in northern Virginia.

---

[13] *Op. cit.*, p. 4.

If Stearns waited until reaching Sandy Creek to form his church, that fact would need explanation. Did he reject the notion of a traveling church? Was the company only loosely tied together? Could some of Stearns' party besides the Marshalls and the Breeds have been unaffiliated with his church in Connecticut, and were they converted during their journey southward? We know only that every one of the company of sixteen was counted a charter member at the formation of the Sandy Creek Church.

Of course, all agreed who should become minister. Stearns was the natural leader and a matchless preacher. But he would not carry all of the responsibilities; the church also chose Daniel Marshall and Joseph Breed, neither as yet ordained, as assistant ministers. A small church, to be sure, to have three ministers, but this church felt that three ministers would not be too many for the program it contemplated.

Elder Stearns began to preach in his new meetinghouse as soon as its pulpit was set in place. The singing of the little congregation sounded far around. Soon people were coming from neighboring farms to hear the first preaching they had heard in months or even years. And they were quick to acknowledge that never in their lifetime had they heard such preaching as that of Shubal Stearns. They could not decide which was the more remarkable, the content or the delivery. Both were excitingly new.

The message of the preacher, in a word, was a simple gospel, easily understood even by rude frontiersmen. Pungent words and homely illustrations made vividly clear some of the profoundest religious ideas.

The inhabitants of the region reckoned themselves Christians, but somehow they had never heard the doctrine of the new birth which Stearns preached with such vigor. Religion to the man of this frontier community was at best a system of rules and restraints, necessary but dull. Its manifestation as the power of God was a strange phenomenon.

The enthusiastic manner of the preaching, too, was unprecedented. Stearns' delivery was warm and appealing, full of persuasive zeal, not at all the commonplace, lecture-type discourses which the people had formerly heard. Strong gestures and a fervent plea told the people that the preacher was intensely involved in his message. It was obvious that he wanted a verdict.

The preacher's deep feeling and personality passed to the members of the church and from them to the visitors. The music in the little pastor's voice soon penetrated every heart, and his piercing, discursive eye seemed to peer into every soul. The tears, tremblings, and shouts of the members quickly affected the visitors, and from the little meetinghouse a tumult of grief at sin and joy at salvation ascended to heaven. Men who came to the meetings to mock returned home praising and glorifying God. The church began to grow!

Then the Separates knew that they had found their home and that God's will was being perfected in them. The heart of their little community held a plan worthy of the heart of an empire.

3
The Promised Land: Its Possession Begun

NEWCOMERS WERE fast filling up central North Carolina in 1755 when Shubal Stearns and his followers arrived. Most of the twenty to thirty thousand inhabitants of the central and western counties had arrived in the previous ten years. Some large tracts of land, twelve thousand acres or more, had been patented by wealthy citizens of the coastal plain, but many farmers claimed small tracts convenient enough to care for personally. These small farmers tended to group together in neighborhoods, and between the neighborhoods stretched extensive reaches of unoccupied land.[1]

The flat land east of the Yadkin was counted most desirable by newcomers. It provided good pasturage for cattle and an abundance of game. The ground was reasonably fertile and the climate generally temperate.

In addition to the movement of people from the coastal region of North Carolina, many emigrants were coming from Virginia, Maryland, and Pennsylvania in a southerly movement. It is true that the French and Indian War disrupted the migration temporarily, although a considerable wave of people came from the valley of Virginia as a direct result of the war. Certainly, the tide was not held back long by this struggle. Moreover, the population grew rapidly by natural increase. Large families of ten or twelve children were common among the vigorous folk who were conquering the new land.

---

[1] G. W. Paschal, *History of North Carolina Baptists* (Raleigh: General Board of North Carolina Baptist State Convention, 1930), I, 252-54.

Indeed, all of North Carolina was in a ferment of growth. By 1755 the total population of the province numbered nearly a hundred thousand, four-fifths of which was white.[2] A large proportion of the early settlers who had come from Virginia represented dissenting religious sentiment. Many of them were refugees from ecclesiastical oppression. Early in the colonial period North Carolina gained a reputation as an asylum for the religiously persecuted. This reputation was advertised widely in England as well as in the colonies. During the proprietary period, dissenters apparently came in larger numbers from Nansemond County, Virginia, than from any other area of similar size. They usually arrived in small companies.

The seat of government for the province in 1755 was New Bern, although the Assembly convened in Wilmington. Since the autumn of 1754, the Governor's Palace in New Bern had been occupied by Arthur Dobbs, the appointee of King George II. Dobbs was soon acquainted with the independent and restless character of his people and with the large problems of the scattered populace. He learned quickly that the people in widely separated settlements of the vast forest of midland and upland Carolina were usually restive under the weight of taxation and authority. They had little money, however abundant their food supply, and for roads they had only footpaths running from settlement to settlement, marked by notches in the trees. To the governor, the people of the interior must have seemed quite remote.

The Church of England had been established by law in 1701 upon motion of Dr. Thomas Bray of the English Society for the Propagation of the Gospel, but it had had only a feeble career in North Carolina. The end of the proprietary period of the colony in 1729 found not a single Anglican minister there. The proprietary charter granted dissenters liberty of conscience and of worship, and this liberty was continued after 1729 as well.

The Society for the Propagation of the Gospel had sent its first two missionaries to North Carolina in 1708; but they had met

---

[2] *Ibid.,* pp. 240-41.

The Promised Land: Its Possession Begun

with hostility. They were poorly maintained by the vestries, and their mission was adjudged a failure. John Urmstone followed them in 1710 and fared only slightly better. About a dozen ministers had been sent during the proprietary period, but they left the province very much as they had found it—religiously apathetic and bankrupt.[3]

After 1729, Governors Burrington and Johnston, predecessors of Dobbs, had tried without success to promote Anglicanism in the Assembly. There was no regularly settled minister of the Church of England in the province during the entire administration of Burrington, and Johnston reported in 1739 but two places of regular Anglican worship. Indifference and hostility toward Anglican ministers was general among the North Carolina people.[4]

When Governor Dobbs arrived in 1754, only one Anglican minister was at work in the province, but he soon had two co-laborers in James Reed at New Bern and John McDowell at Wilmington. A widespread Anglican ministry did not develop, however, before the termination of Dobbs's career. A justice of the peace had to conduct the governor's funeral in 1765.[5]

The earliest dissenters of North Carolina were Quakers. A Quaker William Edmundson supposedly preached the first sermon heard in North Carolina, in 1672. He was closely followed by the founder of Quakerism, George Fox, who spent nineteen days preaching in the Albemarle region in 1672. With this beginning, the followers of Fox became the largest body of Christians in the province during the proprietary period. Their influence extended into politics until 1701, when they were forced out of the Assembly and the Church of England was given the status of the established religion. In view of its early advantage, Quakerism might have continued as the primary religious influence in the region except for its poverty of organization, its dependence upon an itinerant ministry, and its lack of missionary vision.

---

[3] *Ibid.*, p. 122.
[4] *Ibid.*, pp. 242-43.
[5] *Ibid.*, p. 251.

Religious concerns among the many early dissenters were doomed to steady decline because of the shortage of churches, religious instruction, and pastors. The Quakers and the Moravians, however, were exceptions to this until past the middle of the eighteenth century.

There can be little doubt of the wisdom of Shubal Stearns in choosing North Carolina for his missionary labors. The region was a veritable religious vacuum. Its untaught people were in need of spiritual moorings. Since they were religiously indifferent or had rejected orthodox Anglicanism as sterile and foreign to their way of life, they needed a more radical and functional type of Christianity. They would listen to almost any itinerant preacher who came their way with the gospel. Their exterior roughness and lack of religiosity, not to mention the grosser forms of their lawlessness, could not conceal their religious earnestness and their quest for life's meaning.

But was Stearns as wise in selecting the specific site on Sandy Creek for his base of operations as in choosing the larger area for his ministry? What were the prospects for a fruitful ministry in the immediate vicinity of the forks of the Cape Fear River? It is important to note the religious temper of his neighbors in answering these questions.

Quakers came first to conduct organized Christian worship in central North Carolina. Their settlement stood twenty miles east of Sandy Creek on Cane Creek, near the present village of Snow Camp. A monthly meeting was held here at least as early as December, 1751. They had another settlement twenty miles to the north at New Garden (the present site of Guilford College). These communities had their own teachers and traveling brethren.[6]

Forty miles to the northwest, on the Yadkin River, lived the Moravians, a German pietist group with an episcopal church polity. The Moravians began to settle in 1753 on a hundred-thousand-acre tract around the site of the present city of Winston-

---

[6] G. W. Paschal, "Shubal Stearns," *Review and Expositor*, XXXVI (1939), 47.

Salem. Coming in small groups at first, they numbered five hundred people in six settlements by 1776. They brought their own ministers, who, however, could not minister effectively to their English-speaking neighbors because of the language barrier.

West and north of Sandy Creek, and also to the south, were scattered groups of Scotch-Irish Presbyterians, who spoke Gaelic and had no settled ministers.[7] Large numbers of them were found in Cumberland County, where their school teachers sometimes performed the work of ministers, reading sermons and catechizing the children. In Guilford, Alamance, Chatham, and Randolph counties, and in the vacant lands to the east and west of the Yadkin lived occasional groups of German Lutherans and Reformed. They occupied the frontier places before 1750; thereafter, the Scotch-Irish began to settle west of them. The Germans did not speak English, and like the Scotch-Irish they had no settled ministers before 1770.

It would appear, then, that Sandy Creek was surrounded by groups who could not or would not receive the Separates' message. On two sides were people who could not understand English— the Scotch-Irish in Cumberland and Germans in Randolph and Guilford. To the barriers of language and culture were added the barriers of previous denominational commitment. Only toward the east did there seem to be an area open to evangelization, and here several Quaker settlements stood. But if a straight line were drawn eastward for a hundred miles, no church or settled minister of any faith would have been encountered. Beyond the hundred miles, some General Baptists lived.

On the other hand, the Sandy Creek area was fast filling with English-speaking newcomers, most of whom were totally uncommitted to any Christian faith. They were becoming a more important element of the population than all of the foreign-speaking elements combined. Swarming in from regions north of the

---

[7] Scottish Presbyterians had lived in eastern Carolina, especially in Duplin County, at least since 1736. These spoke English and had churches and pastors. They had a meeting house in Orange County by 1736. Paschal, *History*, I, 259-60.

Carolinas, they were quickly transforming the forests and the lands. These people traveled to the region along three forest paths. One, called the Settlers Road, ran from north to south all the way from Pennsylvania to South Carolina. Another, later called Boone Trail, went from Wilmington westward to the Yadkin settlements. And a third, known as the Trading Path, ran from southeastern Virginia (Norfolk) to the Waxhaw country. The three trails converged at Sandy Creek, which promised to become the busiest crossroads of the entire southern frontier. What a strategic site for a church! Pioneers might pass through Sandy Creek but once, but this would give them an opportunity to hear the gospel. Before they should press on to the wilderness they must hear the preaching of the grace of God. Enough people already were passing that way in 1755 to excite the imagination of the little evangelistic church.

The church probably had a modicum of organization at first. Its life was built around its dynamic little leader, and at his side stood two assistants. But the fault of an organization too simple was soon remedied, for, as Semple has noted, Stearns was a specialist in matters of church government and discipline.[8] The pastor held a high and typically Baptist view of the church, and from the first he encouraged active, responsible participation from each member of the fellowship. "All had a word or a prayer or an exhortation."[9] Young converts witnessed immediately after their conversion. Women prayed and spoke freely in public. All the church felt the call to a vast evangelistic ministry.

In accordance with his conviction that a church should closely follow Scripture patterns in organization as in conduct, the pastor began a literal copying of New Testament rites and offices as the church elaborated its structure. Ruling elders, elderesses, deacons, and deaconesses were duly appointed. Nine Christian rites came to be observed at Sandy Creek: baptism, the Lord's Supper, the love feast, laying on of hands, the washing of feet, anointing of

---

[8] *Op. cit.*, p. 6.
[9] Paschal, "Shubal Stearns," p. 50.

The Promised Land: Its Possession Begun 39

the sick, the right hand of fellowship, the kiss of charity, and devoting children.[10] A strict church discipline, practiced from the first, went far toward preserving the moral character of the people in this frontier region.

In all of his leadership, Stearns demonstrated the truth of Morgan Edwards' estimate of him that he was a "man of good natural parts and sound judgment." He had "but a small share" of learning, "yet was pretty well acquainted with books." Undoubtedly, his greatest natural gift was his voice, which was "musical and strong, which he managed in such a manner as, one while, to make soft impressions on the heart, and fetch tears from the eyes in a mechanical way; and anon, to shake the very nerves and throw the animal system into tumults and perturbations."[11] His character was above reproach, and all looked upon him as a father.

Daniel Marshall did not possess such conspicuous gifts as Stearns; he was certainly not as effective a preacher. Morgan Edwards characterized him as "a weak man, a stammerer, no scholar."[12] But his even zeal quickly gained him a reputation for tirelessness, and his enthusiasm and diligence never wavered. Less is known about Joseph Breed, but it is supposed that he possessed much the same character.

Morgan Edwards was right when he said in 1772 that the North Carolina Separate Baptist preachers resembled the Separates of New England "in tones of voice and actions of body; and the people in crying-out under the ministry, falling down as in fits, and awaking in extacies; and both ministers and people resemble those in regarding impulses, visions, and revelations."[13] They

---

[10] In separate churches growing out of Sandy Creek, however, the particular rites to be observed were left to the discretion of the congregations. The number of rites in use varied with the churches.
[11] *North Carolina Historical Review* (Raleigh: North Carolina Historical Society, 1930), VII, 386.
[12] Morgan Edwards, "Materials Towards a History of the Baptists in the Provinces of Maryland, Virginia, North Carolina, South Carolina, Georgia" (MS in the Furman University Library, Greenville, S. C.), VI, 1.
[13] *Op. cit.*, IV, 145.

were indeed a product of the Great Awakening both in the method and content of their preaching. Like Whitefield, they "had acquired a very warm and pathetic address, accompanied by strong gestures and a singular tone of voice."[14]

Stearns' "zealous, animating manner" of preaching at Sandy Creek quickly attracted attention. At first, it was received with considerable suspicion. Men asked whether this were not a strange way indeed to proclaim the gospel. The people found in his "manner, tone of voice, and earnestness," that which they had never seen or heard before.[15] As Edwards quaintly recorded, "the neighborhood was alarmed and the Spirit of God listed to blow as a mighty rushing wind."[16]

Stearns' preaching was prophetic and personal, but its charismatic quality was most notable. The preacher evidenced complete dependence upon the Holy Spirit, and his auditors could not fail to be aware of this. Scarcely a person attended the early Sandy Creek meetings without being conscious of the spiritual influence which pervaded the place. New converts would immediately join in the work of exhortation. Women and children, as well as men, were called upon to testify, and all joined with perfect freedom in obeying the impulses of the Spirit. They experienced fear and trembling, shouting and acclamation, weeping and rejoicing. Much noise and great confusion often prevailed. There was intense religious excitement, if not excessive or uncontrolled conduct.

The evangelist repeatedly called men to hear and obey the gospel. In a short time, he had won the confidence of many. There was a note of authority and urgency in all that he said which won respect. Those who professed conversion were not rushed into the church, but they were tested by the congregation. Some who professed conversion were never admitted.

Word of the Sandy Creek meetings reached neighboring settlements, and invitations came to Stearns to preach. He and his

---

[14] Semple, *op. cit.*, p. 4.
[15] Paschal, *History*, I, 289.
[16] Paschal, "Shubal Stearns," p. 47.

The Promised Land: Its Possession Begun

assistants hastened to answer these messages. As the calls multiplied, some coming from distant settlements, Stearns was careful to give preference to the most neglected neighborhoods. He delighted to preach to the poorest of folk and took no pay for his services.

James Younger, an unordained Welsh Baptist preacher formerly of Welsh Neck settlement in South Carolina, was then living in the Abbott's Creek community a few miles west of Sandy Creek and heard about the Separate Baptist preaching. He traveled to Sandy Creek and returned with Daniel Marshall. It is likely that Stearns also went to Abbott's Creek on a preaching mission. Since Stearns was the only ordained minister among the Separates, he baptized all of the converts.[17] Their number must have been large, for Marshall considered moving to Abbott's Creek to organize them into a church.

The first year at Sandy Creek had not passed before Stearns and Marshall decided to attempt a much larger mission. Facing eastward, the direction which seemed most promising, they would go on a preaching tour all the way to New Bern and the coast. The journey, which was to test public reaction to them, was greeted by enthusiasm beyond their anticipations. Apparently, the entire country through which they passed was aroused. It was recorded that "there was no little enthusiasm among their converts, and they and their followers became known in this section as the Enthusiastical Sect."[18] The people of the coastal region had difficulty identifying the Separate Baptists. Some called them Methodists, but George Whitefield, who visited New Bern in 1755, argued that they could not possibly be Methodists. Governor Dobbs called them "strollers," and Rev. Joseph Reed called them "strolling preachers imported from New England."

It must have been on this first tour of the east that John Newton

---

[17] It soon became customary for a church to appoint a committee who would visit branch communities and "sit as a church" to receive new members. Robert I. Devin, *A History of Grassy Creek Baptist Church* (Raleigh, 1880), p. 72.

[18] *North Carolina Historical Review*, VII, 392 ff.

was won by the preachers. He may have already been a General Baptist preacher, who quietly adopted the views of the Separates. He was not ordained until March, 1757, when he became pastor of Black River Church, Duplin County; but he entered at once upon his ministry as a pioneer Separate Baptist preacher. Ezekiel Hunter, of New River, may have had the same experience.

The year 1756, which saw steady activity by the Separates at Sandy Creek, was marked by several events of great promise. Marshall spent much time on Abbott's Creek, but early in the year he went northward to the Grassy Creek community in the northern part of Granville County. It is likely that he was invited by a small General Baptist group which had been formed as early as 1754. He found that the congregation had a meetinghouse. His preaching was so effective that transformation of the group into a Separate Baptist community was begun. Among the converts was James Reed, soon to become pastor of the church at Grassy Creek and a pioneer of the Separate movement northward. "Father" Stearns went north to baptize him and the other converts.

Stearns conducted a successful evangelistic campaign at Deep River in Chatham County and formed a group of disciples. When two of these, Nathaniel Powell and James Turner, heard of some Baptist fishermen living near the mouth of the Cape Fear River, close to the South Carolina line, they set out to investigate. These fishermen had come with a colony from Cape May, New Jersey, about 1755. They were Particular Baptists formerly with the Philadelphia Association, but they lacked a ministry. Having appealed to the Sandy Creek people, they welcomed Powell and Turner, who convinced them to become Separate Baptists. The Cape Fear people later became the Lockwood's Folly Church.[19]

Stearns and Marshall may have made another trip to the coast in 1756 or 1757. It is likely that they had preached in half a dozen eastern Carolina counties by 1757. John Dillahunty, formerly a Roman Catholic of Maryland, then sheriff at New Bern, was struck by the preaching of George Whitefield near his

---

[19] Paschal, *History*, I, 325.

home in 1755. It is recorded that Stearns and Marshall appeared soon after this in his neighborhood. Dillahunty's wife persuaded him to attend a meeting. Husband and wife were converted, and they were baptized later by Philip Mulkey. Dillahunty became a deacon and later a Separate Baptist minister.[20]

December, 1756 saw the accession to the Sandy Creek ranks of several young men who were to become among the most prominent leaders of the movement. Philip Mulkey, who had been converted near Roanoke in Halifax County, under the ministry of John Newton, was baptized near Christmas time. The Murphy brothers Joseph and William also were baptized; they would soon lead churches in the Carolinas, Virginia, and Tennessee.

The year 1757 marked the formal expansion of church organization beyond Sandy Creek. Daniel Marshall might have constituted his Abbott's Creek group into an autonomous church much earlier but for the problem of his own ordination. Pastor Stearns felt that no church should be formally constituted as long as it was led by an unordained leader. The branches of Sandy Creek could not become churches until ordained pastors were found.

Furthermore, Stearns held that a presbytery of ministers was essential to an ordination service. Here he faced a dilemma, especially in the case of Marshall his brother-in-law, who had fully proven his gifts. Stearns himself was the only ordained minister among the Separates in the South. He hesitated only a short while before calling upon a Particular Baptist preacher on the Pee Dee for assistance, but Stearns was rebuffed. The Particular preacher considered the noisy Separate meetings in which women and ignorant men exhorted as disorderly. At length, Stearns was able to get a message through to a brother-in-law in South Carolina, Henry Leadbetter, who was also an ordained Particular Baptist minister. After Leadbetter came to Abbott's Creek and participated in Marshall's ordination, the work of constituting Abbott's Creek Church proceeded late in 1756 or early in 1757.[21]

---
[20] *Ibid.*, pp. 305-306.
[21] Paschal, *History*, II, 178.

By October, 1757, attractive young Philip Mulkey had gathered the people at Deep River, Chatham County, and was ready to be ordained as their pastor. He thus became minister to the third Separate Baptist church.

In the next year, Daniel Marshall pushed northward into Virginia, the young preachers James Reed, William and Joseph Murphy, and Dutton Lane at his side. They were well received.

Within three years[22] of the Separates' settlement at Sandy Creek there were three fully constituted churches with a combined membership of over nine hundred. Vigorous branches thrived in the region of Sandy Creek at Little River in Montgomery County and Grassy Creek in Granville County, and other branches were located well to the eastward at Southwest in Lenoir County, Black River in Duplin, New River in Onslow, and as far away as Lockwood's Folly in Brunswick. Preaching had been carried on from the Moravian settlements to the Cape Fear and northward into Virginia.

A set of bright young evangelists appeared during the first three years, and their branches sent out other branches, often before a minister was ordained. Colaborers with Stearns, Marshall, and Mulkey, elders of the constituted churches, were James Reed, of Grassy Creek; John Newton, of Black River; Joseph Breed, of Little River; and Ezekiel Hunter, of New River. Charles Markland, of New River, was working at Southwest,[23] and Nathaniel Powell and James Turner, of Deep River, were transforming the Lockwood's Folly people. The evangelists were beginning to occupy the land of promise.

An important step in that direction was taken in 1758 when the Sandy Creek Association was organized. As soon as more than one church appeared, the statesmanlike Stearns, in true Baptist fashion, began plans to draw the churches into a voluntary as-

---

[22] Cf. Henry Sheets, *A History of the Liberty Baptist Association* (Raleigh, 1907), p.1.

[23] Paschal, however, does not believe that Markland left New River for Southwest until about 1760. *N. C. Historical Review*, VII, 391.

sociational relationship. His doctrine of the church would not permit the churches to live independently of and isolated from one another. In Semple's words, he "conceived that an association composed of delegates from all would have a tendency to impart stability, regularity and uniformity to the whole."[24]

Stearns consulted his churches on an association, paying a personal visit to each church and some of their branches. Apparently, a preliminary meeting was held in January, 1758, and the larger organizational gathering occurred in June. The plan required careful planning, for the associational movement would usher in a grand new chapter in Separate Baptist expansion.

---

[24] *Op. cit.*, p. 6.

4

Brush Fires in All Directions

THE FIRST MEETING of the Sandy Creek Association was a great success. It had been widely advertised, and crowds of people thronged to Sandy Creek in June, 1758, many of them out of curiosity. The little meetinghouse overflowed. At least six congregations were represented: Sandy Creek, Abbott's Creek, Deep River, Grassy Creek, New River, and Black River. It is probable that several of these had not yet been constituted as churches.

The meeting did not bother with organizational procedures and the transaction of business. It did not even go so far as to elect a moderator, although everyone looked to Elder Stearns as the man in charge. The order of the day was preaching and exhorting, singing and recounting successes. The only contemporary account of this meeting is the following brief statement of James Reed of Grassy Creek:

> At our first Association we continued together three or four days; great crowds of people attended, mostly through curiosity. The great power of God was among us; the preaching every day seemed to be attended with God's blessing. We carried on our Association with sweet decorum and fellowship to the end. Then we took our leave of one another with many solemn charges from our reverend old father, Shubal Stearns, to stand fast unto the end.[1]

The associational gathering excited the preachers to unprecedented zeal. It sent them back to their places of labor in hot haste to preach the gospel of salvation. It also opened new doors of

---
[1] Devin, *op. cit.*, p. 53.

opportunity, for many who had attended out of curiosity begged the associated churches to send preachers to their neighborhoods. The Separates agreed that no call was to go unheeded. Since they decided that associational meetings should be annual affairs, they set the second Sunday in October as the regular time to convene.

The mother church at Sandy Creek set the pace of growth at the outset. Within a few years, how many is unknown, the membership climbed from the original sixteen to over six hundred.[2] But the missionary outreach of the church was even more remarkable than its growth.

The details of the missionary strategy devised by the Sandy Creek leaders remains a secret, but a careful plan for overspreading the entire surrounding country with gospel preaching evidently was set in motion. Stearns, Marshall, and Mulkey often traveled together, especially on missions to the east, but each man may have accepted a particular direction. Marshall did his best early work, beyond his pastorate at Abbott's Creek, to the northward. Mulkey gave himself for a few years to the southeastern and eastern movement. Stearns, exercising all the while a general oversight over all regions, may have done his most effective itinerating in the east and to the west of Sandy Creek. Other preachers also had special areas of responsibility. That the revival movement reached with almost equal effectiveness toward east and west, north, and south is remarkable. Of course, the islands of non-English speaking people and the Quakers would be generally unaffected. The neighboring Moravians noted and praised the zeal of the Separates, recording that "the Baptists are the only ones in the country who go far and wide preaching and caring for souls."[3]

When Daniel Marshall turned northward to minister in the Grassy Creek community, he found a most productive field of labor. A tireless emissary, he did not hesitate to use extraordinary

---
[2] Semple, *op. cit.*, pp. 3-4.
[3] Paschal, *History*, II, 33.

methods to gather a crowd. He would preach at a muster, a sale, a wedding, or a barn-raising. Conversions, and entire communities stirred by his preaching almost always followed. The Grassy Creek Church was revived and began to grow rapidly. People were attracted to the church from distances of fifty miles or more; some were residents of Virginia.

James Reed, then in his early thirties, was one of the first fruits of Marshall's labors at Grassy Creek. He was baptized in 1756. At the time of his conversion he was illiterate, but under the instruction of his wife, he soon was learning. At first, he was thought "unqualified to instruct in spiritual things," but he was free to recount his own salvation. Exercising his limited talents, Reed quickly gained a reputation as an evangelist. When the Grassy Creek church was constituted in 1762, he was made pastor; and he continued in that capacity for over twenty-five years, retiring in 1789.[4]

Under Reed's ministry the church claimed many of the outstanding families of the region. In this respect it was unique, for the early Separate churches generally were made up of poor and obscure people. Among the early Sandy Creek converts were Jeremiah Walker and Dutton Lane, who were destined to become prominent ministers in North Carolina and Virginia. Lane assumed leadership of Dan River Church, the first Separate church in Virginia in 1760.

The most notable convert in this area, however, was not won directly as a result of Marshall's preaching. He was Samuel Harris, called "The Apostle of Virginia." Harris was born into a home of some prominence in Hanover County, Virginia, in 1724. He was educated "in a manner suitable to his fortune" and as a young man settled in that part of Halifax County, Virginia, which later became Pittsylvania. There he achieved distinction, serving at various times as church warden, sheriff, justice of the peace, colonel of the county, captain and commissary of Fort Mayo and its military garrison. He held most of these posts at the age of

---

[4] Devin, *op. cit.*, p. 85.

thirty-four, when he entered a stage of deep soul searching, "without his knowing why or wherefore," as Morgan Edwards said.[5] The conviction lay heavily upon him that he was a helpless sinner.

When Harris heard that the Murphy brothers of North Carolina were preaching at a private house near Allen's Creek, on the road from Booker's Ferry on the Staunton River to Pittsylvania Court House, he decided to hear them. Riding up in his splendid military uniform, he could scarcely escape notice, but he quietly took a seat in a corner behind a loom. As the sermon progressed, his distress increased, and he pulled off his sword and other military equipment. When the people arose for prayers, they observed that Colonel Harris was on his knees, his head and hands hanging limply down. Hastening to his relief, they found him unconscious. But he soon arose, smiled, and began to cry, "Glory, glory, glory!" From that moment on Harris never doubted his salvation.[6]

Harris was baptized by Daniel Marshall and quickly associated with the branch of Grassy Creek Church which had assembled on Dan River under the leadership of Dutton Lane. The name of so important a citizen gave the Separate Baptist movement a momentous lift in Virginia, for he was the first person of prominence to join the Separates in that state.

Harris' early ministry of seven or eight years was in the Pittsylvania area, where he was made a ruling elder in 1759. His home became a meeting place for the Dan River Church, which was constituted in 1760. When he accepted the office of evangelist in 1769 and toured Virginia northward to the Potomac River, Harris became the most effective evangelistic preacher of his region. Mission trips took him into the Carolinas, and he often traveled with Marshall and imitated his preaching. During much of his ministerial career he also served as pastor of the Falls Creek Church. Two of his brothers were leaders in the Grassy Creek Church, sixty miles from his place of residence.[7]

---

[5] *Op. cit.*, III, 58.
[6] Taylor, *op. cit.*, p. 29.
[7] Devin, *op. cit.*, pp. 55-57.

Stearns, Marshall, and Mulkey, the three ordained ministers, made frequent visits to the eastern part of North Carolina. They preached to all the territory from New Bern to the South Carolina line. Their principal lieutenants in this region appear to have been John Newton and Ezekiel Hunter. As a result of their efforts, churches appeared at Southwest, Trent, Neuse, New River, Black River, and Lockwood's Folly.

Southwest was begun by Charles Markland, of New River. A Sandy Creek presbytery constituted a church there in October, 1762. Lockwood's Folly became an arm of the New River Church, following the visit of Ezekiel Hunter in 1762. It may have become a church the same year.

Hunter was foremost among all the preachers stationed in the eastern part of the state. After he had become pastor of New River Church, Onslow County, in 1759, he itinerated widely throughout his own county and into Duplin, Sampson, New Hanover, and Carteret. He also organized branches at White Swamp in Bladen County and at Livingstone's Creek in Brunswick. His zeal in Onslow made the county almost entirely Baptist. Fame of the revival enthusiasm there spread throughout eastern North Carolina. In 1761 the Anglican Rev. Alexander Stewart spoke of Onslow as "the seat of enthusiasm in this Province." He said that he had preached twice to "the few remaining Episcopalians there."[8]

The established church showed undisguised alarm at Baptist growth in this area. In 1759 New Hanover County church leaders praised their minister Rev. Michael Smith for his great efforts to "curb (if possible) an Enthusiastic sect which call themselves Anabaptists which is numerous" and daily increasing in his parish.[9] In fact, the Separate Baptists were undermining the Anglican church when they convinced people that the baptism of unconverted children was unscriptural. The church depended for its

---

[8] *Colonial Records,* III, 291 ff. and VI, 562, as quoted in *N. C. Historical Review.*

[9] *Colonial Records,* VI, 307, as quoted in Paschal, *History,* Vol. I.

growth upon christening and teaching small children; it almost never baptized adult converts. Now the Episcopal preachers began to itinerate and to immerse adults, but they continued to complain that the people were "bewitched" by Baptist preaching. Their pamphleteering and other propaganda for infant baptism were given a boost in 1764 when George Whitefield stopped briefly in New Bern and spoke against the "rebaptism" of adults and in favor of the baptism of infants.[10]

In the east, by 1762, the Separates must have had at least half a dozen churches, with numerous branches. The warmest enthusiasm pervaded many communities where Baptist preaching was found. The Anglicans were not the only group being displaced by the Baptists, if we are to believe Woodmason's report about this region:

And by their address and assiduity (the Anabaptists) have wormed the Presbyterians out of all their strongholds and drove them away. So that the Baptists are now the most numerous and formidable body of people which the church has to encounter with in the interior and back parts of the Province and the antipathy the two Sects bear each other is astonishing. Wherefore a Presbyterian would sooner marry ten of his children to members of the Church of England than one to a Baptist. The same from the Baptists as to Presbyterians—their rancor is surprising. . . But the Baptists have great prevalence and footing in North Carolina and have taken such deep root there that it will require long time and pains to grub up the layers.[11]

The Baptist movement showed significant expansion to the south and west in the period around 1760, although it involved the dissolution of several of the oldest churches. One of these, Deep River, disappeared as a result of its pioneering and missionary spirit. Apparently, the church was dissolved by common consent. Philip Mulkey, minister since 1757, moved with eight members to the Little River, a tributary of the Broad, where they formed a church in August, 1760. It appears that they combined there

---
[10] *Ibid.*, p. 313.
[11] *Ibid.*, VII, 331 ff.

with a small group under Joseph Breed, who probably never was ordained. Within two years they had one hundred members.[12]

Mulkey's church, not long content with its resting place, moved on in 1762 to the Broad River in South Carolina. Then the original thirteen of the migrating church moved on in December to Fairforest, a tract in the fork between Fairforest Creek and Tyger River. Mulkey continued as pastor of the Fairforest people at least through 1776. By 1772 the church ministered to three hundred families, had one hundred and sixty-seven members, and four branches.[13]

In 1760 one of the Murphy brothers, Joseph, was ordained with the help of Stearns. Early that year he led seven other members of the disbanded Deep River Church to Anson County (later Montgomery), where they settled on a branch of the Pee Dee and formed a church named Little River. On arriving they found some worshipers, probably a branch of Sandy Creek Church, and included them within the fellowship. In three years it had sent out four branches and built five meeting houses! Murphy, who was said to have been "no scholar," but very popular, continued as pastor until 1769, when political differences between him and his people forced him to move westward across the Yadkin near the old Jersey settlement. There he organized Shallow Fords Church from remnants of Gano's Regular Baptist Church. Up and down the Yadkin he went, organizing churches and serving as the only resident English-speaking minister in the area until after the Revolution.[14]

Meanwhile, thirteen remaining members at Deep River moved to Chatham County, where they formed Haw River Church (near Bynum, N. C.), in October, 1764. Pastor of the group was Elnathan Davis, a former Seventh-Day Baptist of Virginia, who had moved to the Haw River section in 1757. His conversion was as dramatic as that of Samuel Harris.

---

[12] *Ibid.*, p. 294. *N. C. Historical Review*, VII, 386 ff.

[13] Leah Townsend, *South Carolina Baptists, 1670-1805* (Florence, S. C.: Florence Printing Co., 1935), p. 126.

[14] *N. C. Historical Review*, VII, 388.

Stearns was holding meetings in the neighborhood. Young Davis and eight or ten rowdy companions went to see Stearns baptize a large man. Davis crept closer to the preacher than his companions were willing to follow. As Stearns preached, Davis saw people tremble. When he drew close to them to examine their condition, one man turned and cried on his shoulder. Davis fled to his friends and told them that a "trembling and crying spirit" was among the people, whether of God or the devil he did not know. In spite of his resolution not to return, Stearns' voice drew him once more into the crowd. Then he was seized with a trembling and sank to the ground. He was burdened with a terrifying sense of sin until he found relief by faith in Christ several days later. He began to preach at once. He was baptized by Stearns and ordained in a service presided over by Samuel Harris, in November, 1764. He led the Haw River Church in such an ambitious extension program that by 1772 it had six branches.

Within a year after Philip Mulkey went to South Carolina, Daniel Marshall and a good portion of his Abbott's Creek membership moved to the same state. Marshall left Abbott's Creek not only because he felt circumscribed by the Sandy Creek Church and the Moravians at Wachovia but also because of unsettled political conditions. He reached Broad River in South Carolina before the end of 1760. Then in 1762 his company moved on to Stevens Creek, where they built a meetinghouse ten miles from Augusta, Georgia. Marshall continued to itinerate, establishing branches on Beaver Creek and across the provincial line in Georgia. Stevens Creek was constituted in 1766 by Marshall, who by that time had gathered and inspired a promising group of young preachers, including his son Abraham, Benjamin Harry, Saunders Walker, and John Herndon. The elder Marshall, Harry, and Walker were very active itinerants.

The back country of South Carolina was fast filling with people who came mostly from North Carolina and Virginia after 1750. Mulkey, Marshall, and their preachers were present to welcome them. Baptist churches began to spring up: Tyger River Church (sixteen miles southeast of Spartanburg) about 1765; Little River Church on Little River of Broad in 1770; Little River of Saluda in 1770 (constituted by Samuel Harris and James Childs, largely of Virginians); Encore Church in 1772; and Congaree Church in 1776.

Mulkey, then Marshall, preached in the Congaree section. Joseph Murphy came down to constitute the Congaree Church. Among the early converts were four who became preachers: John Newton, Thomas Norris, Timothy Dargan, and Joseph Reese.

Reese, like Mulkey, was eloquent and passionate as a preacher. He was preaching in the Little Saluda River area by 1776, where he organized the Mine Creek Church, with the help of Harris and Childs, in 1770. By 1769 he was arousing great enthusiasm in the High Hills of the Santee section. Here he numbered among his converts prominent people such as Dr. Joseph Howard, Thomas Neal, Lewis Collins, and Richard Furman.

Furman was but sixteen years of age when he began to preach regularly. He took charge of the High Hills Church, a branch of the Congaree, in 1774 and later became the greatest figure of his time among Southern Baptists.[15]

The Separates were taking the South Carolina back country; their churches extended to within a hundred miles of Charleston. The churches were drawn together into the Congaree Association in 1771. By 1772 the Separates claimed fully half of the Baptist membership of the province, although the Regulars had been there nearly a century ahead of them. Within twenty more years the Separates were to be far in the lead.

Effects of the Separates' work are indicated in a report by Mr. Woodmason of St. Mark's Parish in 1771:

Religion and the Chh lye bleeding—Wounded ev'ry day—overrun with Sectaries, especially ye New Light Baptists—who have broke up ev'ry Congregation I have founded—All the whole Back Cty is now lost to ye Church thro' want of Ministers & Churches . . . . the

---

[15] Townsend, *op. cit.*, pp. 122 ff.

Vestry of this Psh pressed me to . . . lay aside all thoughts of quitting the Province—to wch I consented, on Acct of ye Number of Baptist Teachers wch had lately appeared amg them.[16]

Daniel Marshall had so much instant success in his forays into Georgia that Lieutenant Governor Bull encouraged the Anglican minister in Augusta to preach in New Windsor, hoping "it will effectively put a stop to the progress of those Baptist vagrants, who continually endeavour to Subvert all order, and make the Minds of the people Giddy, with that which neither they nor their teachers understand."[17]

At one time, Marshall was arrested, convicted, and commanded to preach no more in Georgia. Not only did he continue but also his wife asserted publicly that the authorities were interfering with the preaching of the gospel, quoting Scripture to sustain her view. A young man named Cartledge was convicted by her words and became a minister. Also, the arresting constable and even the magistrate who had tried Marshall were soon converted and baptized![18]

The Georgia field was so promising that Daniel Marshall left his home on Horse Creek, South Carolina, fifteen miles from Augusta, and moved to Kiokee Creek, Georgia, in January 1771. There he formed the first Baptist church in Georgia at Appling in 1772.

Back in North Carolina after 1760, Shubal Stearns must have known lonely moments at the thought that nine of the original sixteen members of Sandy Creek had gone south to stay. Daniel Marshall and his wife, Joseph Breed and his wife, Ezenezer Stearns and his wife, Enos Stinson and his wife, and Peter Stearns all had gone to South Carolina and Georgia.

But Stearns was far too busy to remain nostalgic. He was busy with home pastoral duties, and he was often away from home

---

[16] *Ibid.*, p. 272.
[17] *Ibid.*, p. 124.
[18] J. H. Kilpatrick. *The Baptists* (Atlanta: Georgia Baptist Convention, 1911), pp. 37-38.

officiating at ordination services, helping to constitute churches, and preaching in revival meetings. The tireless little man was aging now, but his pace did not slacken. He did not hesitate to journey to Virginia or South Carolina when called. And there were plenty of calls. The third session of the Sandy Creek Association, in 1760, heard reports of an unprecedented demand for the gospel.[19] By the fifth or sixth session, Separate Baptist preachers were to be found from the mountains to the ocean in North Carolina. And although some people still called them "Ranting Anabaptists," they were a force to be reckoned with.

Devin describes some methods used by the early Separates in their revivals:

At the close of the sermon, the minister would come down from the pulpit and while singing a suitable hymn would go around among the brethren shaking hands. The hymn being sung, he would then extend an invitation to such persons as felt themselves poor guilty sinners, and were anxiously inquiring the way of salvation, to come forward and kneel near the stand, or if they preferred, they could kneel at their seats, proffering to unite with them in prayer for their conversion. After prayer, singing, and exhortation, prolonged according to circumstances, the congregation would be dismissed to meet again at night . . . for preaching or prayer meeting. They held afternoon or night meetings during the week. In these night meetings there would occasionally be preaching, but generally they were only for prayer, praise, and exhortation, and direct personal conversation with those who might be concerned about their soul's salvation.[20]

Stearns' enthusiasm for his revival meetings is clearly expressed in a letter of his to Connecticut on October 16, 1765 about a series of meetings:

The Lord carries on his work gloriously in sundry places in this province, and in Virginia, and in South Carolina. . . . Not long since, I attended a meeting on Hoy (Haw) River, about thirty miles from hence. About seven hundred souls attended the meeting, which held

---

[19] Semple, *op. cit.*, p. 45.
[20] *Op. cit.*, p. 69.

six days. We received twenty-four persons by a satisfactory declaration of grace, and eighteen of them were baptized. The power of God was wonderful.[21]

The power of God was indeed present wherever Stearns went, and his preachers showed the same power. Morgan Edwards gave testimony to this effect when he wrote in 1772, "I believe a preternatural and invisible hand works in the assemblies of the Separate-Baptists bearing down the human mind, as was the case in primitive churches. 1 Cor. xiv. 25."[22]

By 1770 Shubal Stearns had to face the painful necessity of seeing his beloved Sandy Creek Association divide into three parts. He must have known long of the inconvenience to brethren in Virginia and South Carolina who had to come the long distance to Sandy Creek for the annual meeting. But a far more pressing reason to divide was an objection to the degree of authority the Association was exercising over the churches. If Stearns was party to this development, it is hard to understand. He had rebelled years before against the authority of consociations in Connecticut and had stood for a pure congregationalism in a free and voluntary associational life.

The usurpations of local power against which the churches protested concerned in part the "unfellowshipping" of ordinations. In this matter Stearns' error might be partly condoned. He always regarded with extreme care who should be ordained to the ministry. He laid hands hastily on no candidate, for he wanted him first to prove his gifts and calling. In the period of widespread and rapid growth, however, some churches became impatient to have ministers and proceeded to ordain men newly converted to the Christian faith. Naturally, the associational leaders, having Stearns' high view of ministerial standards, were slow to recognize these hasty ordinations. In some cases, they did not recognize the ordinands as ministers.

---

[21] Backus, *History of Baptists*, p. 228.
[22] *N. C. Historical Review*, VII, 385. Separate is misspelled "Separte."

On the other hand, that the Association sometimes disfellowshiped churches for organizing independently, that is, without the supervision of an official associational committee, was less excusable. It went so far as to plead "that though the compleat power be in every church yet every church can transfer it to an association."[23] Interdependence obviously placed some limitations upon local independence, but this limitation was too stringent. It is understandable that disagreement might have come as result of the refusal of an associational committee to constitute a church or to recognize a minister; but, more than disagreement, a principle was involved in the theory of associational authority announced. The churches properly took umbrage, for they felt the limitations too keenly.

Benedict suggests that Stearns "was not wholly divested of those maxims which he had imbibed from the traditions of his fathers,"[24] and perhaps this is true. Some of his spiritual sons, however, had no desire to cling to those maxims. The Virginia Association in the first year of its life unanimously moved to deny associational authority over the churches.[25]

The messengers came to the 1771 meeting of the Sandy Creek Association at Grassy Creek in anything but a good mood. It was customary for the association to act only with unanimity. It soon became apparent that little could be done by that rule on this occasion. They could not agree even on a moderator. In times past when there had been disagreement, the parties had labored in argument, then had resorted to prayer, and, in some cases, had appointed days of fasting and prayer in the attempt to come to one mind. All of these methods failed in 1771. Agreement could be had on one matter only—the association should divide. And so it was agreed. The North Carolina association kept the Sandy Creek name, the South Carolina association called itself the Congaree (after the name of the church in which it first met), and

---

[23] *Ibid.*, p. 399.
[24] *Op. cit.*, p. 53.
[25] *N. C. Historical Review*, VII, 399 ff.

the Virginia group took the name General Association of the Separate Baptists of Virginia.[26]

On November 20, 1771, "reverend old father" Shubal Stearns died amid his labors at the age of sixty-five. His sixteen-year mission to the South was completed. He was the chief light and the guiding genius behind the Separate Baptist movement. There can be no doubt that he planted well, for forty-two churches and one hundred and twenty-five ministers had sprung from the Sandy Creek Church by 1772. The Baptist movement had been securely planted from the Potomac River southward into Georgia, from the Atlantic westward to the mountains. Rarely has a religious leader seen such rapid and magnificent results from a few years of labor. Surely the Lord was in it.

It should be marked, however, that in North Carolina itself Separate Baptist churches were not actually so numerous in 1771. There were many branches of the existing churches, but emigration had taken a heavy toll of church life.[27] Some of the oldest and strongest churches had been dissolved for this reason. Even Sandy Creek was greatly decimated by 1772. Stearns lived only long enough to see foundations laid in North Carolina and beyond; he saw fires started here and there which would not be quenched. In the confidence that God's fires cannot be put out, he fell asleep.

---

[26] G. H. Ryland, *History of the Baptists of Virginia* (Richmond: Virginia Baptist Board of Missions and Education, 1955), pp. 51-52.

[27] G. W. Purefoy says that there were only nine churches in the Sandy Creek Association in 1771, presumably after the South Carolina and Virginia churches had withdrawn. *History of the Sandy Creek Baptist Association* (New York: Sheldon & Co., 1859), p. 62.

5

Are They Blood Brothers?

THE SEPARATE BAPTISTS were unique among the Christian groups of the South. Their individuality lay not only in their methods but also in their theological understanding and doctrinal emphases. For a quarter of a century their distinctive outlook was to keep them aloof from other groups, including their Baptist neighbors who belonged to different traditions.

Separate Baptists inherited the views of Whitefield. The Great Awakening under his leadership, both in Great Britain and in America, had inclined generally toward the Calvinistic system, but it cannot be said that Whitefield ever taught a systematic theology. He said that he had "never read anything that Calvin wrote," and much of his preaching betrayed this. He set forth views which might or might not form a theological scheme. He held that his doctrines came from no man, but from Christ.

Whitefield was no theologian, and he did not permit speculative thought to trouble him. As W. W. Sweet says, "The doctrine of predestination and election never bothered him in his eloquent efforts at soul saving."[1] There was even something of "an unbecoming pride of ignorance" about him. He put little trust in scholars and did not pretend to be an intellectual. Rather, he was a prophet, basing his authority upon the Bible and repeating a few great biblical ideas over and over again.[2]

Whitefield's sermons often began with the doctrine of total depravity. He sometimes declared that "man is half a Devil and half a Beast." The Fall had meant the ruin of man, completely

---

[1] W. W. Sweet, *Revivalism in America* (New York: Charles Scribner's Sons, 1944), p. 32.
[2] Henry, *op. cit.*, pp. 95-97.

perverting his will and making him utterly unable to save himself. Thus, man is cast entirely upon God's election for salvation. Such doctrine, the evangelist held, "strikes at the very root of human pride, cuts sinews of free will all to pieces, and brings the poor sinner to lie down at the foot of sovereign grace."[3]

On the other hand, Whitefield evidently believed that man has some ability to turn himself toward God, although salvation is in no sense by works. He taught that a man could turn to Christ without bothering about predestination. He loved to quote Isaac Watts on this: " 'We should go first to the grammar-school of faith and repentance, before we go to the university of predestination': whereas the devil would have them go first to the university to examine whether they were elected or rejected, or no."[4] Election was certain once the marks of the Holy Spirit appeared in one's life.

It is evident, therefore, that Whitefield believed mightily in the new birth and in assurance concerning the new birth. Knowledge of salvation came through the heart, rather than the mind, and grew out of participation in the life of God. Since any man may have this knowledge once he has heard the truth, Whitefield drove himself to declare the truth to as many men as he could possibly reach. There was an overwhelming urgency about his preaching; the door of salvation must be thrown open to every man. Naturally, Whitefield's theology was kept simple so that any man could understand it. Faith was made easier to comprehend than most other preachers had made it.

This was the tradition of the Separate Baptists. The fire and fervor of the Whitefield revival lived on in them. Their teaching centered in individual conversion and regeneration. Conversion was seen as coming not usually through the fellowship of a church or family but through a separate act of God upon the individual.[5]

---
[3] *Ibid.*, p. 105.
[4] *Ibid.*, p. 124.
[5] R. H. Nichols, "The Influence of the American Environment on the Conception of the Church in American Protestantism," *Church History*, XI (1942), 183-84.

62   *Baptist Foundations in the South*

This understanding belonged to most phases of the Great Awakening, although it did not prevent the Separate Baptists in the South from thinking seriously about the nature of the church. It was in this area, therefore, that the doctrine of children in the covenant of grace came under heaviest attack.

Most Separate Baptists were modified Calvinists although they were not systematic theologians. There was considerable variety of belief among them. They avoided the universalist tendencies of some Arminians, but they either rejected or had little to say about the doctrines of predestination, limited atonement, and election of Calvinism. Jesse Mercer, of Georgia, later said that his father Silas Mercer and Jeptha Vining were quite Calvinistic but that Abraham Marshall was "never considered a predestinarian preacher." The latter, son of Daniel Marshall, used to say that "he was short legged and could not wade in such deep water" as the doctrine of predestination. Yet he was considered a low Calvinist.[6]

Shubal Stearns, too, must be classed as a Calvinist, if the preamble of the Sandy Creek Church covenant written around 1757 be his:

Holding believers baptism; the laying on of hands; particular election of grace by the predestination of God in Christ; effectual calling by the Holy Ghost; free justification through the imputed righteousness of Christ, progressive sanctification through God's grace and truth; the final perseverance, or continuance of the saints in grace; the resurrection of these bodies after death, at the day which God has appointed to judge the quick and dead by Jesus Christ, by the power of God and by the resurrection of Christ; and life everlasting. Amen.[7]

Perhaps the confession of faith of the Abbott's Creek Separate Baptist Church in 1783 more faithfully represents a Separate Baptist theology:

Believing the Old and New Testament to be the perfect rule of life

---
[6] Mosteller, "Separate Baptists," pp. 146-47.
[7] Devin, *op. cit.*, p. 43.

and practice and 2ly Repentance from dead works and 3ly Faith towards God and 4ly The doctrine of baptism and 5ly laying on of hands and 6ly the perseverance of saints 7ly the resurrection of the dead and 8ly Eternal judgment.[8]

Separate Baptists emphasized the necessity of the new birth, the authority of the Scriptures, and the leadership of the Holy Spirit in the lives of God's people. The social situation reinforced these distinctive emphases and helped make them acceptable to rugged frontier folk. Thom[9] spoke of the popular demand for "a distinctive symbol and a comparatively formless faith." Many of the southern people found the symbol in believers' baptism and the formless faith in the wide expanse of Bible teaching discovered by the devout soul.

The Separate Baptists were fearful of formal creeds and adopted no official confessions of faith. Creeds stood for the authoritarianism, formalism, and deadness which they had escaped in New England. They were willing to confess their faith verbally to everyone in a language understood by all. They had neither aptitude nor inclination to be heavily theological. The subtleties of speculative thought held no attraction for them.

The Separates soon were made to realize, however, that there were other Baptist groups in the South beside themselves, all rather small, struggling companies. Distinctions among them are important. The group first to appear in North Carolina was the Arminian General Baptists, who had settled briefly in Virginia before coming south. They began their American church life in Isle of Wight and Prince George counties in eastern Virginia around 1700, and they maintained relations with the General Baptists in England, whence they had come. By 1720 economic and political conditions were causing some to move to North Carolina.

Paul Palmer, of Maryland, a General Baptist, settled in Perquiman's Precinct by 1720, and within a few years he was engaging

---

[8] Sheets, *op. cit.*, p. 83.
[9] W. T. Thom, *The Struggle for Religious Freedom in Virginia: The Baptists* (Baltimore: Johns Hopkins Press, 1912), p. 32.

in evangelistic labors in Chowan County, North Carolina. Here he organized a short-lived church in 1727 at Cisco. Palmer helped to form Shiloh Church in 1729, which continued. The immigrating General Baptists settled especially to the south and west of the Roanoke River, but they were to be found here and there throughout the eastern part of the state. An epidemic in Isle of Wight, Virginia, in 1741 or 1742 is said to have caused numbers of General Baptists to move under William Sojourner to the Kehukee Creek area of North Carolina. The group began a very promising movement of evangelization using itinerant preachers. Between 1727 and 1750 about sixteen General Baptist churches were established in North Carolina, some of which had over two hundred members each.[10]

The General Baptist prosperity was more apparent than real, however; for like their brethren in England, they were victimized by internal weaknesses early in the eighteenth century. They were thus ready to yield to more vigorous Baptist groups entering North Carolina around the middle of the century.

Particular (or Calvinistic) Baptists from Maine had appeared in the area of Charleston, South Carolina, as early as 1696. The church in Charleston had ninety members by 1708.[11] The appearance of General Baptists in this congregation led to a rift not long after, and the Calvinistic cause labored to stay alive. Whitefield's ministry in Charleston somewhat revived the group, and a new era dawned when Oliver Hart came as pastor in 1749 or 1750. Hart led in the formation of the Charleston Association in 1751, following the organization of three other churches.

Welsh Neck, South Carolina, Particular Church (first called Pee Dee) was formed in 1738 of people who came from the Welsh Tract in Delaware. Although it was a small church of sixty-six members as late as 1759,[12] it was to exercise great influence in North Carolina Baptist affairs. Robert Williams, of Northampton

---

[10] Paschal, *History*, I, 147-48.
[11] Townsend, *op. cit.*, p. 12.
[12] *Ibid.*, p. 66.

Are They Blood Brothers? 65

County, North Carolina, went to the Pee Dee area in 1745 and imbibed the Calvinistic doctrine there. He returned to his native county in 1750 and spoke convincingly to numbers of his General Baptist friends. His early influence seems to have been upon the Kehukee Church, whose pastor William Wallis he won in 1751.[13] He may have been responsible for James Smart's preaching Calvinism half a year after his conversion at the hands of the General Baptist evangelist Josiah Hart.[14]

When Williams perceived that a large work remained in North Carolina, especially among the General Baptists, he appealed for help to the oldest and largest Baptist association in America, the Philadelphia. Oliver Hart, of Charleston, made a similar appeal for the back country about the same time. This association responded by sending the promising young preacher John Gano on a survey and preaching tour of the region in 1754. Gano had just completed his schooling at New Jersey College and had just been ordained. This was his first assignment. Going straight to Charleston, he returned by way of Tar River into North Carolina. He visited numbers of churches, preaching upon invitation, and interviewed several General Baptist ministers. When Gano returned to Philadelphia to report on the needs of the South, he urged the association to send other ministers into the growing region. Two prominent ministers Benjamin Miller and Peter P. Van Horn soon afterward undertook southern preaching tours.[15]

Late in 1754 or early in 1755, Miller accompanied a colony of people from the area of his church in New Jersey to the Yadkin River in North Carolina. There he apparently organized a church at Jersey Settlement, but he did not continue long there. Both Miller and Van Horn returned to Philadelphia early in 1756. They had spent their time in the South among the General Baptist churches of eastern North Carolina. One by one these churches had been transformed and reorganized: Kehukee and Fishing Creek

---

[13] Paschal, *History*, I, pp. 205-206.
[14] *Ibid.*, p. 205.
[15] *Ibid.*, pp. 205 ff.

churches in December, 1755, Bear Creek and Swift Creek, early in 1756. This work was continued after the departure of the Philadelphia men by Williams, Wallis, and some Welsh Neck preachers, so that by 1759, Lower Fishing Creek, Pasquotank (Shiloh), Falls of Tar, Toisnot, Red Banks, and Great Cohara churches had been reconstituted as Particular Baptist churches.

It must be noted, however, that although the General Baptist cause was overwhelmed, scarcely 5 per cent of the members of the old churches became charter members of the new Particular Baptist churches. The ministers who were won had not been able to carry the conservative laymen with them into the Calvinistic camp. But, as Paschal observes, the churches had largely been "preachers churches." Thus, General Baptist church life now practically ceased. Only three preachers and one or two of the General churches clung to the old views.[16]

The Particular Baptists installed church discipline in their new churches, something which had been almost entirely lacking. They also introduced church covenants which included the major points of a Calvinistic system of theology. These covenants were used extensively to instruct members. The preachers often considered them the sum of all worthwhile religious knowledge.

There is reason to believe that the remaining General Baptist laymen, having rejected Particular Baptist views, were more receptive to the Separate Baptist message. Undoubtedly, they helped constitute some of the earliest Separate churches. General Baptists gave a number of able leaders to the Separate movement.

The Particular Baptists whom Benjamin Miller had organized continued at Jersey Settlement, but without a pastor. When the Charleston Association petitioned Philadelphia in their behalf, John Gano left Morristown, New Jersey, to come to their aid in 1756. Gano ministered at Jersey Settlement for two and a half years. He reconstituted the church, and it joined the Charleston Association in 1759. At the beginning of 1760, however, Indian incursions caused most of the Jersey people to flee to safety, and

---

[16] *Ibid.*, pp. 211-212, 214.

the church died. During its brief career, the Jersey Settlement Church was the nearest Baptist church to Sandy Creek.

One other type of Baptists appeared in North Carolina before the Revolutionary period. This was the nonresistant Dunkards, a group which arose in Germany in 1707 and came to North Carolina by way of Pennsylvania. The Dunkards (today called the Church of the Brethren) are known to have had at least three churches in central North Carolina, but these appear to have become parts of the Separate Baptist movement by 1770.

The foregoing facts are especially interesting when seen in connection with the Separates' early relationships with the other Baptist groups. These associations were particularly helpful to the Separates for the sake of their own self-identification and self-validation.

The first relations that the Separates had with the Particulars of the South were, of course, in northern Virginia. There their enthusiasm met with the disapproval of the Particulars, and their demonstrations were felt to be out of order by a group which was striving to gain respectability in the popular mind. John Leland pointed to the earliest recognizable difference between the two groups when he said that among the Regulars "the work was solemn and rational; but the Separates were the most zealous and the work among them was very noisy."[17] The incompatibility of the two groups encouraged the Separates to move on southward.

After reaching North Carolina, Stearns was rebuffed by the Particular Baptist pastor at Pee Dee (Welsh Neck) when Stearns asked him to assist in the ordination of Daniel Marshall. But Stearns was not the sort to be embittered by such an experience, and he was not incensed at Particular Baptists in general. He immediately called upon another of them, Henry Leadbetter. Thus he proved himself a true disciple of George Whitefield, who would never let denominational lines hinder his ministry.

Daniel Marshall did not hesitate to respond to the call of the

---

[17] W. M. Gewehr, *The Great Awakening in Virginia, 1740-1790* (Durham, N. C.: Duke University Press, 1930), p. 110.

General Baptists of Grassy Creek in 1756, nor was it likely that he hesitated to add them to his movement without rebaptism. Apparently, he did the same with the former Particular Baptists of Cape Fear after 1758, and the former General Baptist church at Tar River, which became Separate in 1761.

When the Sandy Creek Association met for the second time, in 1759, John Gano attended, but whether he came by invitation is not known. Gano probably had not been at Jersey Settlement when the Separates landed at Sandy Creek, but in his two years there he had heard much talk about them. He was received graciously by Elder Stearns, but the young preachers stood aloof from him as though he were not one of them. They had heard also of the revolutionary changes he had wrought among the General Baptists a few years earlier. However, when Gano was invited to preach, he managed to win all the young men by his enthusiastic and polished proclamation of the gospel. Upon his return from this associational meeting, Gano reported to the Philadelphia brethren on the Separates that "doubtless the power of God was among them, that altho' they were rather immethodical, they certainly had the root of the matter at heart."[18] Gano's outstanding personality was such that had he continued at Jersey Settlement, the two groups in North Carolina might have coalesced rapidly.

In the 1760's the Particular Baptists, partly suspicious and jealous of the Separates, occasionally reckoned themselves "Regular Baptists." This name probably was intended to point out the irregularity of the Separates, but it stuck as the popular name for the Particular party. The Regular churches were quickly stimulated by the more aggressive Separate movement, however, and that they should confront one another at close quarters before long was inevitable. The Charleston Regular Association moved first when it sent Oliver Hart and Evan Pugh to an associational meeting of the North Carolina Separates about 1763 to arrange a union with them. The effort failed. Soon after, however, Philip Mulkey attended a meeting of the Charleston Association

---

[18] Semple, *op. cit.*, pp. 44-45.

bearing queries from his Broad River Church about differences between Regulars and Separates.

Separate and Regular Baptist interests faced each other in 1766 in Orange County, Virginia. A party of Separate preachers, including James Reed and Samuel Harris, undertook a preaching journey into Virginia, in response to appeals there. They met the two leading Regular preachers of northern Virginia, David Thomas and John Garrard. The preachers of both parties wanted to unite in evangelistic efforts, but the people who had gathered to hear them preferred the Separates and prevented a union. Thus the Separates and Regulars proceeded with divided preaching and baptismal services. This was a critical moment for the relations of the two movements. Its outcome was a decision to remain apart.

The Regulars were suspicious of the Separates' enthusiasm and irregularity in permitting women and illiterate men to preach. Moreover, as Fristoe said:

The regular Baptists were jealous of the separate Baptists, because, as yet, they never formed nor adopted any system of doctrine, or made any confession of their faith more than verbally; and it was not thought unreasonable, that if they differed from all other denominations why they should not in a fair, open and candid manner make known their principles to the world.[19]

Yet it was the Regulars who steadily sought union with the Separates after 1768. The Ketocton (Virginia) Regular Association sent three messengers to the meeting of the Separate Association in 1769 proposing a union. The three men bore a letter from the Regulars which urged, "We are . . . all New-Lights." But the proposal was narrowly rejected by the Separates who replied: "Excuse us in love; for we are acquainted with our own order but not so well with yours; and if there is a difference we might ignorantly jump into that which might make us rue it."[20]

---
[19] Quoted in Gewehr, *op. cit.*, p. 109.
[20] Edwards, *op. cit.*, III, p. 113.

It was not lack of acquaintance alone which made the Separates wary; they were loath to adopt a confession of faith as the Regulars would have asked. Also, the Separates thought the Regulars had no standards of simple dress and adornment. Their social habits differed.

After 1770 the Kehukee Regular Association (formed in North Carolina in 1769) often raised the issue of union with the Separates. In 1771 this body, sensing the attraction of the Separates for its people, approved communing with the Separates, and they named delegates to pursue union with the Separates. All efforts failed, however, until after the Revolution.

Leaders of the two movements were conscious of the general unity and agreement of Separate and Regular Baptists. And although the conservatism and preoccupation of the Separates prevented formal union, individual and local co-operation was not thereby prevented. Daniel Marshall performed baptisms for the Regular Edmund Botsford in Georgia prior to Botsford's ordination.[21] The Dutchman's Creek (North Carolina) Regular Church invited Separates to share the Supper with them in 1773,[22] and the Grassy Creek Separate Church extended the hand of fellowship to the Bennett's Creek Regular Baptists in 1777.[23] The Separate preachers Reese and Newton even accepted ordination at the hands of South Carolina Regulars in order to work harmoniously with them, but for this they were censured by the Separates.[24]

It was in the providence of God that the Separates went their own way until after the Revolution, for they were thus able to give full attention to the evangelistic task without organizational and doctrinal encumbrances. This delay also gave the Regular Baptists incentive and time for examining their own inner life, for the Separates offered the Regulars a larger challenge as com-

---

[21] Kilpatrick, *op. cit.*, pp. 39-40.
[22] Paschal, *History*, II, 114.
[23] Devin, *op. cit.*, p. 83.
[24] Edwards, *op. cit.*, V, 62 ff.

petitors than they might have offered as members of the same family. The Awakening was permitted to run its full course in the hands of the Separates until it was interrupted by the Revolution.

6

Persecution and Exodus

POLITICAL TROUBLES in North Carolina profoundly affected the Separate Baptist movement after 1765. There is now little doubt that the Baptists there were prime movers in a contest for liberty which was both a prelude to, and a part of, the American Revolution. When the government of North Carolina tried to suppress the Separate Baptists, it succeeded only in spreading their movement all along the southern frontier. Sandy Creek died as the center of the movement, and Baptist growth in central North Carolina was halted for some years; but the Baptists of that region and of other parts of the province were scattered over a vast area. True to their character, they preached as they went.

By mid-eighteenth century, a distinct cleavage had appeared in North Carolina between the prosperous and aristocratic class of citizens of the east and the poorer, democratic population of the frontier counties. Pioneers had sought the frontier in order to secure a larger freedom than they had known in older communities, for they naturally feared governmental control. Since many settlers had learned to look upon North Carolina as a sanctuary for liberty-loving and oppressed people, they were soon disillusioned by the extension of stringent governmental burdens upon their new communities. Thus a large popular protest arose against what appeared to the people of the central and western counties as illegal interference and oppressive injustice from the general government and its agents. Tension and conflict existed until they were eclipsed by the larger issues of the Revolutionary struggle. They are reflected in Morgan Edwards' characterization of North Carolina in 1772 as "a poor and unhappy province, where supe-

Persecution and Exodus 73

riors make complaints of the people, and the people of their superiors."[1]

The climax of the frontier movement was the so-called War of the Regulation in 1771, when a brief armed conflict broke out. The Regulators, as the frontiersmen called themselves, were not revolutionaries or lovers of disorder, but they were men zealous for liberty and justice. Causes of the Regulator movement include unlawful exaction of taxes under color of legislative authority, unlawful exaction of fees by clerks and county registers of deeds, unequal distribution of the burdens and benefits of government, unequal incidence of taxation, the land policy of Lord Granville's district, and the scarcity of money.[2]

Protests against heavy taxation were published in Granville, Brunswick, and Cumberland counties in 1765, and others came from Orange County in 1766. These documents complained that officers and lawyers extorted more money than the law allowed, that the people paid in taxes between twenty and thirty thousand pounds more "than would sink their paper money, and yet about sixty thousand of it still remained unsunk," and that "neither the governors, proclamations nor prosecutions in civil courts remedied or abated the oppressions."[3] All agreed that more than enough taxes had been collected to pay off the public debt, but still the tax continued.

The provincial Assembly was dominated and controlled by eastern planters. The governor lived in the east. His council, entirely from the east, like himself had no real sympathy with the great democratic population of the interior. Representation in the assembly was tragically disproportionate. The inland county of Orange had more taxables and paid more taxes than any county, but it had only two representatives. Seven eastern counties, with a total white population approximately equal to that of Orange, had fourteen assemblymen.[4] The eastern counties were smaller

---
[1] *Op. cit.,* IV, 1.
[2] Paschal, *History,* I, 367.
[3] *N. C. Historical Review,* VII, 385.
[4] Paschal, *History,* I, 368.

and more prosperous. A third of the white population of the province in the days of Governor Tryon was represented by only eight of the seventy-two assemblymen. This third lived in the frontier counties.

The tax system failed in many ways. The principal source of government income was a poll tax which was levied equally upon the poor and the rich. The revenues were spent largely in the east, where the currency of the province chiefly circulated. Money was very scarce in the western counties. It was scarce enough in the east, but the Assembly helped remedy the situation there by establishing produce warehouses and issuing certificates for stored produce which served as money.[5] When the poorer citizens could not pay their taxes, their lands often were sold hastily at public auction.

Sheriffs, judges, and other officials of county government, all appointees of the governor, were notorious for their injustice. In the western counties they were, as a rule, dishonest, haughty, and overbearing. They pocketed over half of the tax money they collected. Treasurers held public money and used it in private speculations. Sheriffs' embezzlements in 1767 alone amounted to $200,000.[6] Officials scorned the poor and took advantage of the ignorant. The corruption of local officials and the frustration of efforts to secure redress of grievances upon appeal to higher authority, more than anything else, drove the frontier people to desperate measures.

Grievances had been mounting for some years prior to 1765, but when William Tryon became governor in May of that year, the troubles moved quickly toward a crisis. The first activity of a regulator group began as early as 1758, in Rowan County. This county, created out of Anson County only in 1753, was rapidly filling with immigrants in 1768. Its new citizens had come this far west to escape aristocratic officers and wealthy landlords. They wanted the freedom and opportunity which the unoccupied country

---

[5] *Ibid.*
[6] *North Carolina Baptist Historical Papers*, II (April, 1898), 137 ff.

had promised. But as soon as the county was created, a swarm of officers from eastern North Carolina appeared. After 1754 poll and vestry taxes were imposed upon the newcomers and all the rest.

Now, most of the people of Rowan County felt as strongly about the vestry tax as about the persons whom it was intended to support. Almost all of the people were dissenters, most of them Baptists. Religious interests are clearly indicated in the report of the first regulator meeting which was preserved in the Bethabara Diary of the Moravians, September 23, 1758. The diary records that a "mob" about seven hundred strong met near Salisbury, close by Jersey Baptist Church. This spontaneous gathering apparently had no permanent organization. The Moravian diary quotes William Churton, Lord Granville's chief surveyor, that the mob put its demands into certain articles. One article demanded that "the Vestries should be abolished and that each denomination should pay its own ministers."[7] The Vestry Act had been in force for three years, but no Anglican minister had appeared in Rowan County. The people opposed vestry acts on principle, especially since they received no ministerial benefits.

John Gano, the Regular Baptist preacher at Jersey Settlement, may well have been present at the first meeting of the new movement, which took the name of Regulators only in 1768.[8] The aggrieved citizens thus chose a name which would clearly tell their purpose of regulating or reforming local political conditions. Numbers of dissenters, of course, despaired of reformation and began to move on deeper into the frontier region.

Governor Tryon had been lieutenant governor since 1764 when he was elevated to the governorship in 1765. He entered his new duties with the main objective of strengthening the position of the Church of England in the province. He assumed that the great

---

[7] Adelaide Fries (ed.), *Records of the Moravians in North Carolina* (Raleigh: State Department of Archives and History of North Carolina, 1943), I, 191.
[8] Paschal, *History*, II, 42.

need was to increase the numbers and competency of the clergy. He found only five Anglican clergymen in North Carolina and decided that twenty-seven more were needed immediately.[9] The Bishop of London armed Tryon with the authority of a bishop so that he could exercise direct oversight over the enlisted clergymen. The Assembly quickly passed his act for establishment of the Anglican religion.

Tryon knew that North Carolina was full of sectaries, but he believed that approved Anglican ministers could soon win them. The people had run after sectarian preachers, he held, only because of the scarcity of the Anglican clergy. He knew about the aggressiveness of the Separate Baptists, whom he shortly was to call "enemies to society and a scandal to common sense." He supposed at first that they concentrated in the eastern part of the province along the coast, but as he became better informed he was shocked to learn that they were even more numerous in the west.

Tryon's program for his church went badly from the first. He recruited some ministers, but they, in many cases, were badly received in the communities they meant to serve. Many of them gave up and left their posts. Even the Anglican church members hated Tryon's arbitrariness. The sectaries lost nothing, however, and they continued to grow. Tryon's marriage act of 1766 was an act of repression against dissenters, whose ministers, except for Presbyterians, were forbidden to perform the ceremony. But the Baptists were numerous enough to defy the law, and their preachers continued to conduct weddings for which no fee was paid to the governor or the established church. Tryon's wrath against the Baptists grew steadily.

The year 1766 saw an increased tax on the western people. Tryon asked the Assembly for $15,000 for a capitol building, and the Assembly voted the money for "Tryon's Palace" that year. The money had to be raised by heavier taxes. Reaction from the upland counties was not long in coming. When it came, Tryon

---

[9] *Ibid.*, p. 347.

Persecution and Exodus 77

was angered by it and may have planned to suppress the "mob" of Baptists and Quakers whom he believed organized the opposition.

A paper read publicly in Hillsboro in the summer of 1766 called for permanent organizations of citizens, similar to the Sons of Liberty which had resisted successfully the Stamp Act of Great Britain. The first such organization apparently was formed at Sandy Creek at the plantation next to that of Shubal Stearns. Its leader was Herman Husbands, Stearn's neighbor.

Tryon began raising a military force in 1767, ostensibly to deal with the Cherokee Indians. He spent much time training his troops, which he levied greatly from the Presbyterian districts. It appeared good policy to set one group of dissenters against another, the Presbyterians against the Baptists. During a peaceful expedition to treat with the Cherokees, Tryon visited the Moravian settlements on September 18-21, 1767. He represented the Regulators to the Moravians as a rebellious "faction of Baptists and Quakers" and succeeded in convincing some influential brethren. He also secured information from them about their Baptist neighbors. By the time Tryon left, he had the Moravians thoroughly alarmed over the activities of the Regulators.

Late in 1767 and early in 1768 the Regulators observed Orange County closely. Here Edmund Fanning carried on an autocratic and corrupt regime. He was judge of Superior Court, register of deeds, and colonel of militia for the large area now embraced in Rockingham, Caswell, Person, Alamance, Orange, Durham, and Chatham counties, and also parts of Guilford, Randolph, and Wake. Since he had a reputation of mercilessness for the poor, he could claim little good will from the people. His officers were no better.

When Fanning set about to collect additional taxes for Tryon's Palace, he was met by a wave of protests. The people knew that the planters and merchants of eastern North Carolina had resisted successfully the Stamp Act of George III; why, they asked, could not the farmers of Orange, Granville, Anson, and Rowan counties resist the overtaxation and other injustices of a man like Edmund Fanning. The number of Regulators grew. The use of force was decried by the Regulators, who first asked the officers of Orange County to meet, talk over grievances, and formulate plans for relief. The officers would have nothing to do with such a meeting as proposed. Some Regulators then began to consider the use of force. Shubal Stearns was not among these, holding with Herman Husbands that the only justifiable means of rectifying injustices was the use of petition and public appeal.

In the spring of 1768, the horse of a Regulator was seized by the sheriff of Orange County for back taxes. A crowd assembled in Hillsboro, overpowered the sheriff, and took the horse from him. During the excitement, some shots were fired into Fanning's house as a sign of hostility toward his entire regime. Fanning immediately appealed to the governor for permission to call out the militia of Orange and, if necessary, other counties to suppress the dangerous rebels. Tryon gave word for the troops to be made ready. At the same time, he knew that the Regulators' grievances were real; and although he refused to deal with them directly, he promised them justice. He gave orders forbidding officers in Orange to take unlawful fees, but their corruption continued.

When the troops arrived in the Hillsboro area, they arrested the reputed leaders of the recent troubles: Herman Husbands, a former Quaker and a forceful agitator, and William Butler. Following their arrest angry farmers hastened to town. The prisoners were released at once on bail, and accused rioters were bound over to the September court.

After the Hillsboro crisis many Baptists began to consider leaving the region. The Bethabara Diary for August 24, 1768 reported that "a party of men from Orange County passed through our village. They were Regulators, and said they were going to Holston's River to look for land—though there may be another reason."[10] Thus by 1768 some Baptists had already "despaired of seeing better times, and therefore quitted the Province." The only

---
[10] *Ibid.*, p. 57.

people known to have gone to Holston River (east Tennessee) at this time were Baptists.

At the September, 1768, court at Hillsboro, several accused rioters were fined and imprisoned, but they were later pardoned. The next year, Regulators in this and other counties made charges of misconduct against officers and appealed to the courts. But the appeals were placed into the hands of the very men who were being charged. And since the courts were controlled by the accused, no action was taken. In several places the Regulators yielded to mob spirit, broke up courts, and whipped the officers. Some court records were destroyed.

Meanwhile, the people continued at the mercy of local officials due to Tryon's inactivity. Even when the sheriffs' dishonesty was discovered, they were not removed from office. Clerks of court and registers of deeds continued to extort. Juries and grand juries were packed to obstruct justice. Cliques of officers and their henchmen controlled the election of representatives of the counties in the Assembly. Any citizen who complained to the officers might expect to be maliciously persecuted. Exorbitant fees prevented the people from hiring attorneys in most cases. There were no newspapers through which the oppressed might state their grievances. Tryon, looking upon complaint as presumptuous, made illegal all assembling for grievances. Edmund Fanning was convicted of extortion in 1768, but he was not removed from office. To permit him to regain a seat in the Assembly, when he had been rejected by popular vote in Orange County, Tryon made the town of Hillsboro a borough. When the court at that place obstructed justice in September, 1770, the Regulators again attacked the court.[11]

When Shubal Stearns, who fully agreed with Regulator aims, saw that the course of the Regulators tended more and more to bloodshed and revolution, he tried to persuade his churches to declare against all use of arms and violence. The Sandy Creek Church actually passed a resolution excluding any member who

---

[11] *Ibid.*, I, 373 ff.

should take up arms against the government. To this action there was an immediate, violent reaction within Regulator ranks and perhaps within the church. A group of Regulators led by two men named Hunter and Butler invaded the meetinghouse and demanded repeal of the resolution. The church rescinded the action.

Stearns did not surrender to the more radical spirits, however, for he soon afterward called for the formation of a new movement among the Regulators to be known as "The Associators," which would oppose all violence. But the appeal of the aged pastor did not suffice to draw from the Regulator movement as a whole any pledge of nonviolence. Beyond the Sandy Creek Baptist congregation, the Associators movement came to nought.

By the spring of 1771, the political disorder had spread over the entire province. Some fifteen counties complained of the government. In some counties armed Regulators defied both the courts and the militia. The Regulators demanded the governor and the Assembly to act at once, but the governor would not convene the Assembly.

The Regulators still wanted a peaceful settlement, but Governor Tryon wanted war. He summarily gained the consent of the council and began to raise forces for overwhelming the "Insurgents." He was more convinced than ever that a rebellious faction of Baptists and Quakers caused the troubles of the frontier counties, and so a vengeful religious enthusiasm spurred him on.

On March 6, 1771, a company of from four to five hundred Regulators encamped in the woods between the town of Salisbury and the Yadkin. When the authorities questioned them, they replied that they wished "only to petition the Court for a redress of Grievances against Officers taking exorbitant Fees." They said that they did not intend to disturb the court and that such arms as some of them carried were to defend themselves if attacked. Arbitrators were appointed to treat with the governor, and a meeting was set for the third Thursday in May. Then, with some assurance of relief, the men went home.

The arbitrators Frobeck and Martin were able to make no head-

Persecution and Exodus   81

way with the governor, however. Tryon vetoed the entire arbitration scheme. Instead of arbitration, Tryon called out the provincial militia. This force, which was made up entirely of North Carolinians, had as its most prominent officers Hugh Waddell, John Ashe, and Richard Caswell. Tryon sought but failed to secure British regulars for his campaign. He would have a fight anyway, even though the militia had no enthusiasm for it. Meanwhile, orders came transferring him to the governorship of New York, but not even this shook his steadfast purpose.

Tryon issued a manifesto demanding the Regulators either to appear before him or be called traitors, but the Regulators refused. The two forces met at Great Alamance Creek, west of Hillsboro, on May 16, 1771. The Regulators sent messengers to petition Tryon to hear their grievances, but he said that the Regulators must first lay down their arms. When they refused, Tryon ordered, "Disperse or be fired upon." The Regulators retorted, "Fire and be damned."[12]

Thus began the Battle of Alamance between two thousand poorly armed and poorly organized Regulators and somewhat fewer armed and disciplined militiamen. The Regulators had no officers higher than captains, and each company fought independently. Probably, fewer than one thousand Regulators were armed. At first they held their ground, some of their sharpshooters hitting with deadly accuracy; then the tide turned gradually. The battle, which lasted two hours, ended with the rout of the Regulators. Some nine men were killed on each side. Around sixty militiamen were wounded.[13]

Tryon condemned twelve leaders of the insurrection to death and sent his horsemen in all directions to round them up. Except for the leaders, all were promised pardons by the Governor, provided they would take an oath of loyalty and peace. Six thousand

---

[12] Alex M. Arnett, *The Story of North Carolina* (Chapel Hill: University of North Carolina Press, 1933), pp. 195-96.
[13] S. C. Williams, *The Baptists of Tennessee* (Kingsport: Southern Publishers, Inc., 1930), I, 8-9.

took the oath within a period of six weeks. Some leaders were executed, others were pardoned, and still others fled. The Battle of Alamance marked the end of armed resistance by the Regulators. It did not mark the end of Tryon's war with the Baptists.

What part did Baptists play in the War of the Regulation? Morgan Edwards would have his readers believe that few Regulators were Baptist, but as Paschal has clearly shown, this could not have been the case.[14] Baptists formed the largest part of the population in the region for which Alamance was the center. There was no other denominational group which could have provided a large proportion of the Regulators. Anglicans and Presbyterians were scarce there. Also, before the battle, Presbyterian ministers are known to have urged the Regulators to submit to and ally with the Governor.[15] Some Quakers who lived near Alamance were in the so-called mob, but they were few. Moreover, the sympathies and activities of many Baptist Regulators are well known. The Regulator contention for religious equality and freedom was characteristically a Baptist argument. Tryon was probably right when he looked upon Baptist communities as enemy strongholds. Members of this denomination must have formed a good part of the fifty thousand Regulator participants and sympathizers.

Edwards bases his conviction regarding Baptist nonparticipation in the Regulator movement upon the action of the Sandy Creek Association in 1769 which forbade Baptists to take up arms against the government. But even this action did not keep Baptists from becoming Regulators. It is true that the Haw River Church forbade its members to join the Regulators, but many joined anyway. James Billingsley a Sandy Creek exhorter is known to have been a Regulator,[16] although not many other Baptist preachers are known to have been prominent in the movement. Perhaps the most conclusive evidence that Baptists participated

---

[14] *History*, I, 49.
[15] *N. C. Baptist Historical Papers*, pp. 137 ff.
[16] Paschal, *History*, I, 366.

Persecution and Exodus 83

is that most settlers in the region of the Regulator troubles—especially in the section between Haw River and Deep River and south of Cane Creek—were Baptists. These colonial Baptists prized religious and civil liberty above life itself.

The victory at Alamance did not satisfy Governor Tryon. The Baptists were not crushed by the battle. Tryon determined, therefore, to carry out his original scheme of a crusade against the Baptist communities. Immediately to the west of Alamance were Baptist settlements at Sandy Creek, Jersey, Abbott's Creek, Shallow Fords, Deep Creek, Hunting Creek, and Belew's Creek. Here, as Paschal says, was "a larger Baptist population than in any other area of like size in the entire world." Tryon's military force so increased in strength after Alamance that it doubled the number of men who fought for the Governor in that battle. With his enlarged militia, Tryon campaigned through the Baptist communities, ostensibly to round up Regulator leaders. However, he laid waste to plantations, burned homes, and sent numbers of men in chains to Hillsboro. The countryside was terrorized.

Three separate operations were undertaken by the vindictive Governor—to Sandy Creek, to Jersey Settlement, and to the Shallow Fords neighborhood. Each expedition attacked a principal Baptist center. Tryon then led his army to Sandy Creek where he encamped, and he forced the inhabitants to give promises of loyalty. The army lived off the countryside, but the soldiers were restrained in their treatment of citizens. The reason for this mild treatment is said to have been Shubal Stearns' action in urging his people not to fight at Alamance. The Sandy Creek folk, nevertheless, knew a week of terror during the encampment of the army, whose intentions could only be guessed. The week was sufficient to convince most members of Sandy Creek Church that they must migrate.

Then Tryon moved his camp to a point two miles east of Jersey Church, on the road from the Moravian settlements to Hillsboro. This was an ideal location for a bloody war on the Baptists. To the east lay the Abbott's Creek, Uwharrie, and Carraway Creek

Baptist communities. To the west were others at the forks of the Yadkin, Dutchman's Creek, Hunting Creek, and up the Yadkin. Next to Sandy Creek, the strength of the Regulators was greatest in the Yadkin Valley. To the north were still other Baptist groups on Town Creek, Belew's Creek, and the Dan River. Tryon's three divisions now included a large number of volunteers who were friends of Tryon and who hated the Baptists. Edmund Fanning, commander of one division, sent horsemen across the Yadkin to seize Regulators and drag them back to camp. They particularly sought Joseph Murphy, but he slipped away and went up the Yadkin, where he was thought to have hidden in a cave. Benjamin Merrill, on whose farm Tryon encamped, was seized and put to death. He appears to have been a leader in the Jersey Church. In all, some forty men were captured and dragged to Tryon's tent at Merrill's plantation. They were treated as renegades and traitors before trial.

After a week, on June 1, 1771, Tryon's and Waddell's divisions were moved to Bethabara and Salem, in the neighborhood of Shallow Fords. More prisoners were brought in to face Tryon, who sat as their judge. Those he considered outlaws he usually sent ahead of him in chains to Hillsboro. Tryon left Bethabara on June 9, and on July 1 he left North Carolina forever. His fanatical, sanguinary campaign against the Baptists had been carried on as his last enterprise in the region after his election as governor of New York.

The earlier Regulator troubles had caused the Baptists to seek the wilderness from 1768 onward. Political conditions, no doubt, had much to do with the movement of the Deep River and Abbott's Creek churches southward in 1768 and 1769 and of the Orange countymen westward in 1768. Other Baptists followed these pioneers. The Bethabara Diary of September 21, 1771, records that "there were unusually many strangers in our town today, especially a number who do not wish to be under the law, and are moving to Holston River."[17]

---

[17] Fries, *op. cit.*, p. 415.

Persecution and Exodus 85

After Alamance, of course, the Baptists left wholesale. Morgan Edwards reported in 1772 that fifteen hundred families departed straightway and that "a great many more are only waiting to dispose of their plantations in order to follow them." The Alamance region was almost emptied of Baptists and did not recover a considerable Baptist population for a hundred years. Sandy Creek Church in a few years was reduced from six hundred and six members to fourteen by 1772. Little River Church dropped from five hundred members to scarcely a dozen. Tidence Lane and some others from Abbott's Creek went northward into Virginia, but most went south and west. It was as though the Battle of Alamance and the death of Shubal Stearns six months later had been twin signals for most of the Baptist people of central North Carolina to disperse.

The exact journeys of the migrating North Carolina Separates are impossible to trace, but it is known that a majority of the people came to rest on the South Carolina frontier. The newcomers quickly occupied the back country of South Carolina in 1772 and 1773.

Some Separates settled in the hill country of western North Carolina. Among those who pressed through this region, one group from Sandy Creek settled on Boone's Creek (Washington County), Tennessee, probably late in 1771. There they established Buffaloe Church. Soon afterward, other Separate Baptists, whose points of origin cannot be determined, founded two other churches in east Tennessee. The Indian war of 1774 scattered them, but remnants of their membership gathered again after the Revolution and renewed their church life. Thereafter, the exiles would not be dislodged from their mountain valleys.

Thus, Governor Tryon's political despotism and religious intolerance seriously hindered the Separate Baptist movement in North Carolina. Benedict knew of less than thirty Baptist churches there in 1776. However, the dispersion of the Separates south of Sandy Creek spread them abundantly along the South Carolina frontier, while the dispersion of those north of Sandy Creek sent the earliest pioneers to Tennessee. Everywhere the Separates made ideal frontiersmen. They stood ready to preach to the newcomers as the people of the infant nation began to pour in a torrent through the mountain passes on their way west after the Revolution. Tryon succeeded only in spreading the virile seed all along the southern frontier.

7

All Ablaze in Virginia

A VISION of Shubal Stearns has been recorded by Edwards.[1] According to the historian, this vision occurred during a great storm September 7, 1769, about two years before the death of the noble evangelist.

As Stearns was ascending a hill not far from his home, he saw on the horizon "a white heap like snow." As he approached the formation, which appeared to be suspended fifteen or twenty feet above ground, the mass suddenly fell to the ground and broke into three parts. The greatest part moved northward, a second part southward, and the third "less than either but much brighter" remained in the spot where it fell. Stearns watched first the northern part and then the southern as they vanished. Then after he had pondered the meaning of what he had seen, he decided that "the bright heap is our religious interest; which will divide and spread north and south, but chiefly northward; while a small part remains at Sandy Creek." His interpretation was prophetic, for in Virginia the Separate Baptist revival culminated with significant effects upon church and nation.

While the North Carolina Baptists were being buffeted by political animosity and religious persecution, the movement in Virginia was passing through two distinct phases. The first, from 1758 to 1769, was a period of slow but persistent growth in the face of a determined popular hostility. This early opposition to the Baptists came chiefly from the lower classes and was based

---

[1] *Op. cit.*, IV, 28.

upon prejudice of one kind or another. Tradition equated the Baptists with Anabaptism and Anabaptism with radicalism. While many of the common people were disturbed by the strange mannerisms of the preachers, some were shocked by the novelty of their teachings. There was superstitious dread that the revivalists would seize unwilling persons and make a public spectacle of them. It was widely rumored that the Baptist preachers were workers of magic, wolves in sheep's clothing. Many were sure that the loud preaching and noisy meetings hinted at anarchy. Men solemnly vowed never to listen to or take seriously a Baptist preacher. Years were required to dispel these commonly held prejudices.

The second phase of pre-Revolutionary development of the Baptists in Virginia, 1769-75, saw a remarkable conversion of the common man regarding the character and mission of Baptist preachers. The role of reformers and prophets was now popularly assigned to the evangelists. But this phase saw the beginning of a determined official opposition and persecution, as authorities of the established order of church and state sought to preserve the *status quo*. Occasional mob violence was associated with official opposition. Partly as a consequence of this persecution, the Baptist revival reached its zenith and overspread most of the settled areas of Virginia. Then the social aspect of the movement began to alter.

The Virginia expansion was intimately tied up with the career and ministry of Colonel Samuel Harris. Following his baptism in 1758, Harris immediately began to relate his conversion experience and to exhort in the area of his home on Dan River. He always had an eager audience. Resigning from his official positions in the army and the provincial government, he determined to devote his time to the propagation of the gospel. He narrowed his business interests almost to the vanishing point in order to secure freedom for preaching.[2] At the time of his conversion,

---

[2] Edwards claims "he took all his money and threw it away into the bushes," perhaps all he had in his pocket. *Op. cit.*, III, 61.

he was having an impressive new home built, much more commodious than the old one. The roof was scarcely on the new house when he decided that the structure should become the meeting place for his church and that his family would continue to live in the old residence.

Harris' love for the brotherhood knew no bounds, and his generosity to it became celebrated. The church regularly gathered to celebrate the love feast at his home, and he insisted upon providing the food.

Soon after his conversion, the Colonel was impressed with a desire to preach to the officers and men at Fort Mayo. When the chance arrived, he began immediately to urge with great force the necessity of the new birth.

An officer interrupted him: "Colonel, you have sucked much eloquence from the rum cask, today: Pray give us a little; that we may declaim as well, when it comes to our turn."

Harris replied, "I am not drunk," and went on with his message.

Soon another officer stopped him saying, "Sam, you say you are not drunk; pray are you not mad, then? What the devil ails you?"

Harris replied in Paul's words, "I am not mad, most noble gentleman." One of these men was converted by the discourse.[3]

Harris began touring with Daniel Marshall, whose tones and style of preaching he copied. He also itinerated alone, spending the first six or seven years of his ministry principally in his own and neighboring counties. In 1759, the church at Grassy Creek ordained him a ruling elder, that is, an assistant to the minister in spiritual rather than temporal functions.[4] His reputation for piety and charity extended far. His family lived frugally, for he gave most of his wealth to religious work.

On one occasion, according to Semple,[5] a man owed Harris a sum of money at a time when his family actually needed it, but

---

[3] Semple, *op. cit.,* p. 381.
[4] Probably he was given oversight of a branch of the church in Virginia.
[5] *Op. cit.,* pp. 383-84.

the debtor said that he could not pay. When Harris offered to take payment in wheat, of which the debtor had an abundant crop, the man said that he had other uses for his wheat. Moreover, the debtor said that he had no intention of paying until he was sued. Harris left him musing: "Good God, what shall I do? Must I leave preaching to attend to a lawsuit! Perhaps a thousand souls will perish in the meantime, for want of hearing of Jesus."

Harris then decided to sue the man at "the court of heaven," and he turned aside to pray. As he told the story later, "Jesus said unto him, Harris, keep on preaching, and I will become security for the payment." Passing the man's house soon after, he left a receipt with a servant for payment in full of the debt. The debtor soon after demanded an explanation, and Harris told of the court-of-heaven decision. The debt was soon paid.

From the time of his conversion, Harris was a fearless preacher. The excellence of his preaching lay chiefly in "addressing the heart," and Semple holds that "perhaps even Whitefield did not surpass him in this."[6] He was a man of the greatest personal force. He seldom failed to stir an audience, his eyes appearing to pour forth "streams of celestial lightning." People were known to fall before his gaze as though struck by a bolt from heaven. He was commonly spoken of, for this reason, as Boanerges. Like most of the Separate preachers, he was governed by impression, impulse, and feeling. On occasions when he did not have freedom of utterance, he would sit down, telling his audience that he could not preach without the Lord.

Harris had the assistance of several North Carolina itinerants in planting the earliest Separate churches in south central Virginia. The Dan River Church was constituted in 1760 by Daniel Marshall and Philip Mulkey. There were seventy-four charter members, of whom eleven were Negroes. Charter members included Harris, Dutton Lane, Thomas Hargat, and their wives. Perhaps Harris and Lane shared pastoral duties until Lane was ordained in 1764. Branches of the church appeared soon after its constitution.

---

[6] *Ibid.*, p. 380.

All Ablaze in Virginia

An Anglican minister in Lunenburg County reported in 1759 that "wherever the Baptists appeared the people flocked over to them." It is not surprising then that by 1759 Mulkey and William Murphy were able to gather in that county a group of worshipers on the Bluestone River. It was made up largely of Negroes belonging to William Byrd II and did not become a constituted church until 1772.[7]

In 1761 Murphy was ordained and took charge of a church on Staunton River, and in the same year he organized Black Water Church (in present-day Franklin County, Va.). Both churches were made up of newly arrived frontier people. A branch of the Black Water Church lived as far west as the Little River, in what is now Floyd County. Thus six years passed without any known advance by the Separates into interior parts of Virginia.

The call to come northward to the center of the province came surprisingly from a convert of the Regular Baptists in Culpeper County. The Great Awakening had touched the Regulars of northern Virginia, especially after David Thomas' arrival in 1760. Thomas, who had earned the degree of Master of Arts at Rhode Island College and had come under the quickening influence of George Whitefield's preaching, came from Pennsylvania on "a ministerial visit" to Mill Creek Church (now Berkeley County, W. Va.). He stayed on as pastor of the Broad Run Church, constituted in 1762, in Fauquier County, Virginia. His good sense and learning contributed greatly to raising the popular estimation of the Regular Baptists.

Thomas' zeal for the spread of the gospel often sent him on preaching tours to neglected areas of northern Virginia. Allen Wyley, a pious man of Culpeper, heard of Thomas and went to Fauquier to hear him in 1763. He then invited Thomas to preach at his home in Culpeper. But when Thomas attempted to preach there, he was prevented, probably by a mob. He was, however, able to preach effectively in neighboring Orange County.[8]

---

[7] Ryland, *op. cit.*, p. 39.
[8] *Ibid.*, pp. 15-17.

Wyley, however, was determined to have evangelical preaching in his home area; and when he heard of the Separate Baptists in Pittsylvania, he set out in January, 1765, to invite their preachers. He traveled uncertainly in the country of southern Virginia, but, providentially, he was directed to one of Colonel Harris' meetings. Harris saw him as he entered the meeting house and felt at once that the man bore some extraordinary message. As soon as it was convenient, Harris asked him his business. Believing him sent by God, Harris agreed to go with him.

After three days the men started out. They had no preaching appointments on the way, but Harris, as usual, stopped often in homes to pray and exhort. In Culpeper the preaching was not interrupted the first day, but on the second a mob gathered, armed with whips, sticks, and clubs. During the night Harris went over into Orange, where he seems to have preached successfully without serious opposition. Some previously stirred by Regular Baptist preaching clung to his words, and others were awakened for the first time. Harris spent "many days" there, during which time he marked men who seemed to have preaching gifts and advised them to continue the meetings after his leaving. This they did almost daily in a tobacco house where they met. Among the exhorters were the Craig brothers Lewis and Elijah, converts of David Thomas, who later became famous preachers.[9]

The little group in Orange appealed to David Thomas to come as soon as possible to preach for them. Thomas came but expressed disapproval of the preaching by illiterate and unauthorized persons. The people felt rebuffed and decided to send for Harris to return to them. Elijah Craig and two companions started for Harris' home sometime in 1776, but on arriving there, they were surprised to learn that Harris had not been ordained and so could not administer the ordinances. He suggested, however, that they go with him sixty miles into North Carolina to get James Reed. When they reached Reed's residence, they found Reed and a member of his church, Mr. Graves, getting ready to journey to

---

[9] Semple, *op. cit.,* p. 8.

Virginia. Awake and in his dreams Reed recently had felt led to preach in that region, so much so that his family sometimes had heard him cry out in his sleep the name of the province to the north of him.

The entire party, including Reed and Harris, set out for Orange, preaching at many points along the way. Large congregations awaited them in Orange. On their second day there they preached at Elijah Craig's house and there encountered the Regular Baptist preachers David Thomas and John Garrard. However, the Separate and Regular preachers failed to join in a united evangelistic effort. Rather, they went their separate ways, Harris and Reed taking a circuit through Spottsylvania, Caroline, Hanover, and Goochland counties. Reed baptized nineteen converts in Orange the first day and more later, and he and Harris had similar encouragement on their entire tour. They resolved to tour the same region the next year, and they made appointments in advance.

In the absence of Harris and Reed from central Virginia, Lewis Craig went on with his preaching. When he was haled before the Spottsylvania County court and charged with unlawful preaching, he became the first man to suffer at the hands of the law in Virginia's effort to suppress the Separate Baptists. After the grand jury had been dismissed, Semple[10] records, Craig had the temerity to buy each member a mug of grog. Then, having gained their attention, he addressed them: "I thank you, gentlemen of the grand jury, for the honor you have done me. While I was wicked and injurious, you took no notice of me; but since I have altered my course of life, and endeavoured to reform my neighbors, you concern yourselves about me. I have gotten this mug of grog, to treat you with; and shall take the spoiling of my goods joyfully."

One member of the grand jury was young John Waller, called "Swearing Jack" Waller because of his reputation for profanity. He despised the Baptists and considered them a nuisance. The mien and spirit, as well as the words, of Craig attracted Waller, who determined to find out more about Craig's religion. Thus

---
[10] *Ibid.*, p. 45.

he began to attend Baptist meetings. For seven or eight months he despaired of finding the mercy of God; then suddenly he found it.

When Harris and Reed came north in 1767, Waller met them in Orange. Reed baptized him there. Waller then hastened home to sell property for paying off his gambling debts. This business attended to, he began at once to preach that men everywhere ought to repent.

On the same trip northward which witnessed the baptism of Waller, the three preachers Harris, Reed, and Lane assisted in constituting the Upper Spottsylvania Church on November 20, 1767. Twenty-five members made up this first Separate Baptist church north of the James River. Earlier in the year a delegation of leaders from Spottsylvania had attended the meeting of the Sandy Creek Association to request the commissioning of a presbytery to form the church. Harris, Reed, and Lane composed the presbytery.

Young Waller's success as a preacher soon irritated the authorities, and on June 4, 1768, he and four other preachers were arrested at their meetinghouse. In court they were arraigned for disturbing the peace. An accusation of the prosecuting attorney was that they could not "meet a man upon the road, but they must ram a text of scripture down his throat." Reed and William Marsh may have taken advantage of the offer of release on condition they would not preach again in the county for a year and a day. But Waller, Lewis Craig, and James Chiles, all of whom lived in the county, refused and were taken to jail. As they walked through the streets of Fredericksburg to the county jail, they were singing Watts' hymn "Broad Is the Road That Leads to Death." The people who stood by the way did not applaud their imprisonment, for they regarded the preachers with considerable awe. After forty-three days' imprisonment, the men were released, and they returned to their work as heroes in the eyes of many.[11]

Reed and Harris continued to visit the Spottsylvania area

---

[11] *Ibid.*, pp. 403 ff.

All Ablaze in Virginia

regularly for several years, although the journey was three hundred arduous miles. Nowhere else did they have comparable success. On one journey they baptized over two hundred, and on a particular day they baptized seventy-five. Multitudes of people thronged to hear them, hundreds camping on the grounds of the meeting place overnight in order to be present for the next day's meetings. Often the meetings continued far into the night, and after their close the people were loath to go to rest. The preachers might be awakened at any hour of the night by the cries of the penitent. People came fifty, sixty, or even a hundred miles to hear the preachers. There was an intense earnestness about their seeking. What Morgan Edwards said of Harris was true of all the preachers: he "left a train of seriousness after him wherever he went."[12]

In order to accommodate the growing membership, two new churches were constituted in December, 1769—Lower Spottsylvania and Blue Run. John Waller shortly assumed pastoral care of the former, Elijah Craig of the latter, and Lewis Craig became minister of Upper Spottsylvania. The Spottsylvania pastors turned their attention southward to the neighboring counties of Goochland and Louisa, where the Word was committed into the hands of consecrated young converts Reuben Ford, William Webber, and Joseph Anthony.

In the years 1769-71, revival fires were breaking out in all quarters. In northern Virginia a group of religiously concerned people gathered about James Ireland, a schoolmaster, on the Shenandoah River. John Pickett, a dancing teacher and a gambler of neighboring Fauquier County, traveling in North Carolina, encountered the Separate Baptists and returned home a Christian. Word of his evangelizing his neighbors reached the little group on the Shenandoah, who invited him to come over the mountain to preach. Pickett went the sixty miles and preached for two days on experimental religion. He convinced the group of the Baptist way, except that Ireland, a recent immigrant from Scotland, was

---

[12] *Op. cit.*, III, 59.

loath to renounce the Presbyterian practice of infant baptism. These people had Regular Baptist neighbors. When these neighbors, in the name of the Ketocton Association, sent Garrard, Major, and Saunders as a committee of fraternal messengers in 1769 to the Sandy Creek Separate Association in North Carolina, Ireland decided to accompany the committee. He was late in deciding, however, and had to ride hard for 150 miles and cross the James by boat before overtaking the party.

On the way to Sandy Creek, the committee was joined at Amelia by Jeremiah Walker, a North Carolina Separate who had been preaching by invitation on Nottaway River. Walker and Garrard had serious conversations with Ireland as they journeyed.

At the 1769 meeting of the Sandy Creek Association, Samuel Harris was ordained to the ministry. His ordination had been delayed, probably at his own request or possibly because his views of ministerial support were not accepted. Also, he was not yet counted chief minister of any particular church, but he had been giving himself entirely to the work of evangelism. When the Association adjourned, Ireland went with Harris and others to Pittsylvania, where he joined in three days of preaching. Then the Dan River Church heard Ireland's experience and accepted him for baptism. Ireland appears to have been the first person baptized by Samuel Harris. His credentials as an itinerant were then signed by eleven ministers, who rejoiced greatly upon his recruitment.

Harris and Ireland were in northern Virginia by November, 1769, when they constituted Carter's Run Church, made up of people gathered by Ireland on the Shenandoah and Pickett in Fauquier. The first of its kind in this section of Virginia, the church became by 1772 one of the largest Separate churches of the Old Dominion. An early convert of this church was William Marshall, formerly of the Northern Neck, uncle of Chief Justice Marshall. Many were said to have been shocked at the conversion of a man of "so much distinction." When Marshall's preaching in an adjoining area had won fifty-three converts, Harris came two hundred miles to baptize and organize them into the South River Church by 1770. Culpeper Church, in present Rappahannock County, was constituted in 1771, after having been a branch of Carter's Run. By 1770 John Koontz of Front Royal was preaching to the Mennonites on the south fork of the Shenandoah.[13]

In southern Virginia, Jeremiah Walker's Nottoway Church was formed in 1769 in Amelia County, and Harris' Falls Creek Church in 1770 in Pittsylvania. County Line in Pittsylvania, Cub Creek in Charlotte, Meherrin in Lunenburg, and Sandy Creek in Amelia followed in 1771.

In the west, Amherst, Bedford, and Buckingham became Separate organizations in 1771. In the central counties the Spottsylvania preachers were chief instruments in planting Goldmine in Louisa (1770) and Goochland in the county of the same name.

Then, Semple observes, as result of "a spark being struck out," there began "a new flame at a distance" in the extreme eastern part of Virginia. William Mullen, a native of Middlesex, settled in Amelia where he embraced the gospel. On a visit to his relatives in Middlesex and Essex in 1769, he convinced his brother John and his brother-in-law James Greenwood of the necessity of being born again. In November, 1770, John Waller and John Burruss were drawn to preach in this section. Greenwood began to preach. Numbers of converts awaited baptism at the hands of visiting preachers; groups stood ready to be constituted into churches. There was also much Baptist preaching in Caroline County in 1771.

South of the James, there was occasional Baptist preaching in Chesterfield by 1770. Farther south a regiment of young preachers of unusual promise was being raised up in John Williams, Robert Stockton, James Shelbourne, Elijah Baker, Henry Lester, and others.

The heroism of the preachers was sensational. John Waller was

---
[13] Ryland, *op. cit.*, pp. 55-56.

preaching in Caroline in the spring of 1771 when he was rudely interrupted by the minister of the parish, his clerk, and the county sheriff. As Waller prayed, the sheriff thrust the handle of a horsewhip into Waller's mouth and down his throat. Then Waller was pulled down from his preaching place and flogged, without any semblance of a trial. But no sooner was the whipping over than Waller, bloody and disheveled, climbed painfully back onto the speaker's platform and delivered one of the most extraordinary sermons he ever preached. The effect upon the audience was electric; Waller could claim nearly the entire company as disciples.[14]

The organizational meeting of the General Association of Separate Baptists of Virginia was held in May, 1771, at Blue Run (Rapid-ann) meetinghouse in Orange County. A year before there had been only two Separate churches north of the James River, four to the south of it. But now twelve churches were represented, eight north of the James. Three churches were not represented. Samuel Harris was elected first moderator, John Waller first clerk of the Association, which was often spoken of as the "Rapid-ann" or "Orange" Association.

John Williams, of Nottoway, has preserved in his manuscript journal the only record of the proceedings. He reports that following his arrival at 1:00 P.M. on Saturday, "Bro. Hargitt" [Hargate, of Amherst] preached to twelve hundred souls. Immediately after, Burruss preached. As he preached, he "set the Christians all afire with the Love of God; the Assembly praising God with a loud voice." Then Waller exhorted "till he got spent." The "Brothers Marshall and Elijah Craig both broke loose together for half an hour or more, the Christians shouting." After an hour's intermission, officers were chosen and church letters were read; preaching the Word had precedence over business at this first associational meeting.

Sunday was a day of preaching, with William Webber, Jeremiah Walker, Lewis Craig, Samuel Harris, and William Marshall par-

---

[14] Edwards, *op. cit.*, III, 75-76.

ticipating before an audience of from four to five thousand. Monday saw the delegates at the meetinghouse "three hours B' sun!" Harris exhorted before a business session in which Walker contended for a polity of entire local independence but was strongly opposed by the brethren. Lewis Craig, John Young, Nathaniel Saunders, and Reuben Pickett preached to about a thousand. The last day saw debating of business alternating with preaching. A petition was noted from "out-of-doors from five hundred for preaching." Lovell and Williams were appointed to supply the demand, with the result that there was "a good deal of exercise among the people." Debates indoors concerned Arminianism and the civil licensing of preachers. Both matters were referred to the next association.[15]

Positive conclusions of this meeting concerned the following matters:

1. The Association was to be only an advisory council.
2. The Association had the right to withdraw from non-corresponding churches.
3. Members too far from a church to assemble with ease monthly might petition an ordained minister to constitute them.
4. Any ordained man might administer the sacraments and help ordain elders and deacons when called upon.
5. A church in distress should ask sister churches for help.
6. A transgressing delegate might be barred from sitting in the Association.
7. Majority rule was to obtain in the Association.
8. An itinerant minister would be properly recommended by a church, not the Association, and examined by a presbytery.
9. Circular letters would be used by the Association.
10. Each church should use their own liberty about covenanting.
11. An association had no right to dismiss a member from a church or from the Baptist order; discipline was a local prerogative.
12. Terms of communion were fellowship in the same faith and order.[16]

The General Association met next in September, 1771, at

---
[15] Semple, *op. cit.*, pp. 489-91.
[16] *Ibid.*, p. 53.

Thompson's meetinghouse (Goldmine), in Louisa County. Thereafter, two meetings a year became the rule. By 1772 the Separate churches had surpassed in number the churches of their Regular brethren in Virginia. Apparently, fourteen Regular churches with eight branches existed that year, and the Separates counted twenty churches with twenty-one branches. The Regulars had fifteen ministers and ten assistants in the field; the Separates had only eleven full ministers but fifty-three assistants. Some of the churches of the latter had an abundance of ministering brethren. Goochland Church, for example, had six "exhorters" in 1772.[17] As many as forty thousand Virginians may have heard the gospel from the Baptists in that year. John Waller probably was doing the most spectacular work at that time in counties east of Richmond. He organized Lower King and Queen and Glebe Landing churches (King and Queen County) in 1772, the first churches constituted east of Richmond.

Leaders of the established church were alarmed beyond measure at observing the great crowds at the Baptist meetings and the very few people in the parish churches. Without success, they debated with the preachers to refute their views publicly, and they accused the preachers of continuing the radicalism of sixteenth-century German Anabaptism. Finally, numbers of them called upon the civil arm to repress the Baptist movement. In 1772 official persecution of the Baptists broke out in Chesterfield, King and Queen, and Caroline. This was but the beginning of a large-scale and desperate effort by the official order to quell Baptist enthusiasm.

When the General Association met in May, 1773, thirty-four churches were represented. They reported a combined membership of 3,195, of which 526 had been added in the past year. A decision was rendered about the rite of laying on of hands: the churches were "left at their liberty to act as they may think best." Also, Elijah Craig proposed that the association be divided into two districts, one north and the other south of the James River.

---

[17] Edwards, *op. cit.*, III, 85.

At the fall meeting of that year, the division of the association was agreed upon. One of the two annual meetings, however, was to be a joint meeting of the districts, and it would continue the General Association name.

The years 1773 and 1774 saw a remarkable ministry by Elijah Baker, of Lunenburg, in the peninsular area east of Richmond. Baker spent a year after his conversion exhorting in his native community before itinerating in his home county for two more years. Then he "gave up all worldly cares" and went forth to devote his full time to preaching. In the lower end of Henrico County he helped organize Boar Swamp Church. Then he became the pioneer preacher and chief planter of churches in Charles City, James City, York, and Gloucester counties.[18] One of his Gloucester converts, Thomas Elliott, challenged him to go to Elliott's home region, the Eastern Shore of Virginia. He accepted the challenge, and in 1776 Elliott and Baker crossed the Chesapeake Bay and began to tour the rich agricultural region beyond. Baker had phenomenal success in planting churches there.

When the General Association met in May, 1774, both Baptist expansion and persecution of the Baptists were at high tide. Samuel Harris, who had been chosen moderator of both district meetings, was again elected moderator of the Association. The Southern District could now report twenty-seven churches with 2,033 members, while the Northern District had twenty-four churches with 1,921 members. Letters came to the Association from ministers imprisoned for preaching without a license. The Association, therefore, agreed "to set apart the second and third Saturday in June, as public fast days, in behalf of our poor blind persecutors, and for the releasement of our brethren."[19]

Also, the question was raised at this meeting as to whether all of the ministerial gifts of the primitive church ought to be in use at the present time. "A great majority" of the delegates felt that the gifts ought to be in use, but the matter rested until the Southern

---
[18] Semple, *op. cit.*, pp. 395-96.
[19] *Ibid.*, p. 56.

District meeting of October, 1774. There it was decided to supply the primitive offices as qualified men could be found.

Samuel Harris was straightway nominated as "apostle," elected, and ordained to office. He was charged with the work of "pervading" the churches, attending to ordination services, setting things in order in the churches, and reporting to the Association. Care was taken to prescribe discipline for an apostle should such absolute powers permit his becoming an autocrat. He should be dealt with in the church in which the transgression should occur, with the aid of "helps" from two or three neighboring churches. If an apostle were thus judged a transgressor, a general conference of the churches would be called to deal with his case.

At the Northern District meeting, John Waller and Elijah Craig were ordained apostles. The apostles themselves made discouraging reports at the next meeting of the General Association, however, and it was agreed that the office did not "belong to ordinary times." No more apostles were appointed.

There were Separate Baptist churches in twenty-eight of the sixty counties of Virginia by the end of 1774. There was at least one church in every county in which Baptist preachers were imprisoned.[20] A wonderful growth had occurred within a few years, and persecution seems to have had little effect upon it.

By 1775 the upstart Baptists were thinking seriously of challenging not only the established church of Virginia but even the principle of an establishment. Their attacks upon the Anglican church sharpened as they grew boldly critical of its ecclesiastical nature and its corrupt, pleasure-loving clergy, who often led the opposition to the Baptists.

The Separates had greatly stimulated the Regulars in northern Virginia. The Regulars were showing an aggressiveness in some areas, particularly the upper Northern Neck, which would have been a credit to the Separates. One report pointed out that they were "quite destroying pleasure" in Loudoun County.[21]

---

[20] Ryland, *op. cit.*, p. 85.
[21] Semple, *op cit.*, p. 76.

All Ablaze in Virginia

With the coming of the Revolution, the Baptist advance slackened. Separate Baptist leaders became preoccupied with politics, religious liberty, and doctrinal explorations. The May, 1775 General Association learned that only three hundred converts had been baptized since its last meeting. The revival was not over, but tidings of coolness from churches here and there indicated that fires were burning low.

A doctrinal issue as old as Augustine was raised by a query addressed to the May, 1775 General Association: "Is salvation by Christ made possible for every individual of the human race?" A warm debate followed, in which nearly every preacher tried to participate. Those who took an Arminian point of view seemed to have owned the talents and influence, including Samuel Harris, Jeremiah Walker, and John Waller. The Calvinistic viewpoint had very able support from such men as William Murphy, John Williams, and Elijah Craig. When a vote was taken toward the close of the day, it was found that the Calvinists had a small majority.

That evening the Arminians determined to see if their views would be a bar to fellowship, and the next day they learned to their dismay that this seemed to be the case. They then withdrew out of doors, taking the moderator with them. The Calvinists chose John Williams as their moderator. For some time the two groups were separate, communicating by messengers. Finally, the Arminians offered what seemed to be a compromise: "We do not deny the former part of your proposal, respecting particular election of grace, still retaining our liberty, with regard to construction." To this the other party consented, and a happy reunion followed.

This discussion was but one evidence of concern among the Separate Baptists of Virginia for consolidating rapidly made gains in the Old Dominion and for attaining doctrinal stability.

8

Persecution and Struggle for Freedom in Virginia

SEPARATE BAPTISTS assumed the proportions of a significant group at a most critical period of American history. The democratic movement which was to climax in the American Revolution was gathering as a mighty wave at the very time the Baptists were coming to public notice. And while the ferment of political revolution needed the sanctifying idealism and popular support which the Baptists could offer, the Baptists required a political leadership if they were to achieve their most cherished civic end—religious freedom for all.

Skirmishes in the war for religious freedom were fought in the Carolinas and Georgia, in addition to the protracted struggle in New England. Before 1773, there was one case of official persecution of a dissenting preacher in South Carolina, when Joseph Cates a Baptist itinerant was whipped for preaching near Cheraw Hill. When the community resented this act, the authorities tried to justify themselves by claiming that Cates was immoral.[1]

In Georgia, Daniel Marshall was arrested while preaching in the parish of St. Paul. He was convicted and told to preach no more in Georgia. Marshall openly refused, stating that he took his orders from God only. He was seconded by his fearless wife, who quoted Scripture passages pronouncing woes upon those who hinder the preaching of the gospel. There the matter ended, except that the arresting constable, the magistrate who tried Marshall, and a witness named Cartledge were all converted to Baptist views as result.[2]

---

[1] Townsend, *op. cit.,* p. 274.
[2] Kilpatrick, *op. cit.,* pp. 37-38.

It was in Virginia, however, that the decisive phases of the contest for religious freedom in America were fought. Of all the religious denominations in Virginia, the Separate Baptists played by far the most important role in this contest. In the providence of God, they were raised up to bear witness to their distinguishing beliefs and to fight for freedom in a most propitious hour.

In no American colony was the episcopal church system worked out so fully or the Anglican church established so firmly as in Virginia. For a long time other denominations were not tolerated in the colony. A law in 1643 forbade anyone to teach or preach religion, publicly or privately, who was not a minister of the Church of England. The same law instructed governor and council to expel all nonconformists from the colony. Some Puritans who tried to settle in Virginia were obliged to leave in 1649. One hundred and eighteen of them moved into Maryland.[3] When Quakers appeared in Virginia, and did not heed commands to depart at once, they were severely persecuted. By 1655 all heads of households in Virginia were compelled to pay a tithe of fifteen pounds of tobacco per head for ministers' salaries and glebe lands to support the churches.

During the Commonwelath period in England, church affairs in Virginia were in disorder; but by 1661 when the Commonwealth had run its course, the Church of England was again fully reestablished in Virginia. A penalty of fifty pounds of tobacco was assessed upon all who failed to attend services of the established church. The year 1662 saw the passage of a law heavily penalizing parents who refused to have their children christened. The law assessing a fine of two thousand pounds of tobacco was aimed at the Quakers, who continued to appear in the colony from time to time.

For a number of years, Virginia paid scant attention to the English Act of Toleration of 1689, which granted nonconformists a bare toleration; but a few Presbyterian preachers secured state

---

[3] L. P. Little, *Imprisoned Preachers and Religious Liberty in Virginia* (Lynchburg: J. P. Bell Co., 1938), p. 4.

licensing of dissenting preachers and preaching places. Some Presbyterian preachers were licensed in 1692 and again in 1699.[4] General Baptists from England appeared in Virginia around 1700, and since they lived quietly and with little organization, they too were granted a grudging toleration. The Particular (or Regular) Baptists of northern Virginia, after 1752, lived on the frontier and scarcely came to the attention of the authorities. On the whole, Virginia was the province of the Church of England until the Revolutionary period.

In spite of its close alliance with the state, however, the church did not prosper. One reason for this was the inferior quality of clergymen who came to serve the colonial churches. Many of them had come to the New World only after having been adjudged failures in the Church of England. Some were morally corrupt. Since nearly all were brought in from the mother country, they were out of touch with the people of America. The Baptist preachers as indigenes contrasted sharply with the Anglican parsons, who were often men of very limited ability. The parsons' preaching was dull in the extreme, having almost no emotional appeal. Most parsons merely read old moral discourses.

The administrative structure of Anglicanism in Virginia was haphazard and inefficient. In the absence of colonial bishops, local vestries practically strangled the affairs of most of the churches. They regulated, hindered, and nearly starved the parsons, most of whom were at their mercy. Appeals of the parsons to London were ineffectual. There was little incentive for expansion or missionary effort. Churches were far apart, often one to a county. Consequently, many people found church attendance very inconvenient.

Moreover, state sponsorship proved more and more an embarrassment to the Anglican church in Virginia after mid-eighteenth century. The church, like the royal governor, came to be looked upon as the arm of monarchy in a period of democratic and nationalistic idealism.

---

[4] *Ibid.*, pp. 11-12.

The coming of the Separate Baptists to Virginia was ignored at first by the established church. Regarded as a phenomenon of frontier fanaticism, their movement appeared to be a passing fancy unworthy of official notice. Moreover, the lawless element of the frontier was depended upon to crush any religious movement.

The Separate preachers certainly did encounter popular opposition almost as soon as they arrived in Virginia. Mobs prompted sheriffs and others to arrest the preachers. Joseph Murphy was arrested and taken before a magistrate not far from Dan River, but he defended himself so well that the magistrate released him to go about his business.[5] Dutton Lane's preaching at Meherrin was interrupted by a magistrate who charged him not to preach there again. Richard Elkins, an assistant to Lane, was about to be served a warrant by James Roberts in 1769, when Roberts was said to have been blinded by a strange light and prevented from pursuing his purpose.[6]

Samuel Harris on his first mission north of the James was driven from his preaching place in Culpeper in 1765 by a mob armed with sticks, whips, and clubs. Soon after while preaching at Orange, he was pulled down and dragged about by his hair and a leg. More than once pitched battles were fought between his opposers and his supporters, but Harris' reputation, dignified bearing, and boldness often prevented mobs from laying hands on him. In his own county he was never molested.

Mobs heaped indignities upon nearly all of the Separate preachers. Ignorant and superstitious crowds vented their fury upon the nonresisting preachers. Nothing excited the persecutors more than dragging the preachers to mud holes and plunging them in until they nearly drowned. This was considered most apt to ridicule the Baptist mode of baptism. But the Baptists thrived on persecution and even made converts from the mob. Authorities of church and state soon became alarmed at the growth of the revival movement and sought official means to suppress it.

---
[5] *Ibid.,* p. 37.
[6] Taylor, *op. cit.,* p. 30.

The Great Awakening had reached Virginia ahead of the first Separate Baptist preachers. In 1743, Samuel Morris, a citizen of Hanover County, obtained a volume of Whitefield's sermons and began to read from it to his neighbors. Soon the interested neighbors grew too many for his home, so a meetinghouse was erected. Nearby communities invited Morris to read sermons among them. The revival thus begun was guided in the direction of New-side Presbyterianism in 1743 by William Robinson, a graduate of the "Log College" of the Tennant family at Neshaminy, Pennsylvania. The awakened people were dissatisfied with both the lives and the teachings of the established clergymen. Other readers now ministered in a number of neighborhoods. John Blair and John Roan visited the people, and they were followed by William Tennant, Jr. and Samuel Blair, all Presbyterians from New Jersey and Pennsylvania. Finally, brilliant Samuel Davies of New Jersey, another "Log College" man, came to direct the movement. Denied the privilege of itinerant preaching, he secured a license to preach in four meetinghouses. Soon he became pastor of the four congregations.

Under Davies' preaching the revival interest grew to a climax. Both gentlemen and slaves were converted. The alarm and hostility of the authorities were dealt with in part by Davies' assurance to the Anglican Commissary Dawson that he had "no ambition to presbyterianize the colony" but that he wanted only to relieve the sad religious condition in Virginia. The revival declined when Davies closed his mission to the south in 1759.[7]

The Presbyterian awakening had important consequences. It introduced the revival phenomenon to Virginia, created interest in the evangelization of the Negroes, established Presbyterian dissent, and cleared the way for a more aggressive type of evangelism. However, the Presbyterian revival was short-lived, and it affected only a small area in east-central Virginia. By challenging the failure of the Virginia colony fully to apply the Toleration Act, it

---

[7] C. H. Maxton, *The Great Awakening in the Middle Colonies* (Chicago: University of Chicago Press, 1920), pp. 101-102.

rendered notable service and put Presbyterianism in an advantageous position among dissenting groups. The Presbyterians, however, by insisting upon high educational standards for their ministry and upon strict creeds for their people were not able to take the revival to the masses.

As the Presbyterian phase of the revival waned, the Baptists appeared and revived the enthusiasm. They were far more aggressive than the Presbyterians and uninhibited about educational standards for the ministry, emotional display, and a strict creed. They could reach and stir the common people as the Presbyterians never did. Their preachers offered a new type of religious leadership in America. However unacceptable these preachers might have been in the New England meetinghouse or the Presbyterian church, they were ideally suited to a frontier ministry.

By 1759 the authorities were observing a marked change in popular attitude toward the Baptists. Several quarters reported that wherever Baptists appeared the people flocked to them. Churchmen became anxious lest their church be threatened by the rising tide of this radical religious enthusiasm. James Craig, Anglican minister in Lunenburg County, wrote in 1759: "In Halifax one Samuel Harris, formerly Burgess for that County, and one William Murphy have raised and propagated a most shocking Delusion, which threatens the entire subversion of true Religion in these parts, unless the principle persons concerned in that delusion are apprehended or otherwise restrained."[8]

That was the best way to halt the ubiquitous Baptists, it was reasoned—silence their preachers. Thus in various parts of Virginia, county officials, prompted by parsons and others who were zealous for the Anglican church, launched a campaign to put Baptist preachers out of circulation until the religious enthusiasm they had engendered should die down. The campaign was not set in motion officially from the capitol at Williamsburg; it was the work of local officials. Its projection depended very largely upon

---

[8] Ryland, *op. cit.*, pp. 67-68.

the zeal with which county sheriffs and magistrates supported the established church and, in this interest, waged war on the Baptists.

The Virginia statute books had no law which decreed imprisonment for unauthorized preaching, but there was a law requiring the licensing of dissenting preachers. Most Separate Baptist preachers, deriving their authority from God alone, rejected this law. They considered it no business of the state who should or should not preach. They would not apply for licenses.

Actually, it was not easy for a dissenting preacher to secure a license. He needed character references from the parson of his parish and two other prominent citizens. All three might be zealous Anglicans. The Separate preachers were usually itinerants; many had long since left their former places of residence. Who could vouch for their characters and orthodoxy? Also, the applicant had to make the long journey to Williamsburg, since applications had to be approved by the General Court which met only twice yearly. Upon arriving at the capitol, he might have a long delay, as action could be postponed for one reason or another. In the end, the application might be refused, for only one dissenting meetinghouse was licensed for an entire county.[9]

Baptist preachers often were arraigned on the charge of unauthorized preaching, but they were imprisoned for disturbing the peace. The law regarding the licensing of dissenting preachers did not meet the requirements of their persecutors. But the law against disturbing the peace was made to serve the purpose. The preachers were regularly jailed for disturbing the peace.

Lewis Craig appears to have been arraigned in Spottsylvania as early as 1766, soon after his conversion and before his baptism. He was fined by the county court for preaching.[10] The first imprisonments of preachers occurred in 1768. Lewis Craig, John Waller, James Childs, James Reed, and William Marsh were arrested together at Craig's meetinghouse in Spottsylvania, on June 4. Three justices bound them to appear in court two days

---
[9] *Ibid.*
[10] Little, *op. cit.*, p. 35.

later. At court they were charged with disturbing the peace, but Waller confounded the court with his defense. An offer was made to release all of the men if they would promise to preach no more in the county for a year and a day. Reed and Marsh, who were far from their homes and did not expect to preach there soon again, agreed and were set free.

Waller, Childs, and Craig, natives of the county, refused to promise and were jailed. The people regarded them with awe as they walked to prison and, afterwards, flocked to hear them preach from the jail windows. After four weeks the men petitioned for release but were denied. Then Craig entered into a recognizance to carry the petition to the General Court, and he was released to go to Williamsburg. The other men, after spending forty-three days in jail, were released upon receipt of a letter from the acting governor to the king's attorney in Fredericksburg. The common people regarded their discharge as a triumph for the preachers. Great crowds now hastened to hear them without further opposition. Spottsylvania County learned a lesson and never again jailed the Baptists for preaching.

Other counties were slower to learn. Orange imprisoned Elijah Craig for a considerable time in 1768.[11] Culpeper jailed James Ireland in November, 1769, after he had been warned of imprisonment if he preached once more in the county. Released on bail in April, 1770, he rode to Williamsburg with a petition from a number of citizens for the licensing of a Baptist meetinghouse. There the clergy refused to examine him, but he found a country parson for this purpose. The license was granted. Upon his return to Culpeper, Ireland engaged a lawyer who quickly convinced the magistrates who had prosecuted him that they had acted illegally. Court was adjourned.[12]

In 1770 John Pickett spent three months in Fauquier County jail. In December of the same year, William Webber and Joseph Anthony were kept in Chesterfield County jail until March. Their

---
[11] *Ibid.*, p. 145.
[12] *Life of the Rev. James Ireland* (Winchester, Va., 1819), pp. 178-80.

preaching was so effective during their imprisonment that it was "judged the best policy to dismiss" them. The cell door was left unlocked, but they would not escape. Their spiritual reputation became widespread. When the preachers were released from jail, they preached with new fervor and to greater crowds.

A vicious campaign of hate was waged by some defenders of the establishment. The following bit of acrid propaganda appeared in the Virginia *Gazette*, October 31, 1771, entitled "A Receipe to Make an AnaBaptist Preacher in Two Days Time":

Take the Herbs of Hypocracy and Ambition, of each an Handful, of the Spirit of Pride two Drams, of the Seed of Dissention and Discord one Ounce, of the Flower of Formality three Scruples, of the Roots of Stubbornness and Obstinacy four Pounds; and bruise them altogether in the Mortar of Vain-Glory, with the Pestle of Contradiction, putting amongst them one Pint of the Spirit of Self-conceitedness. When it is luke-warm let the Dissenting Brother take two or three Spoonfuls of it, Morning and Evening before Exercise; and while his Mouth is full of the Elestuary he will make a wry Face, wink with his Eyes, and squeeze out some Tears of Dissimulation. Then let him speak as the Spirit of Giddiness gives him Utterance. This will make the Schismatick endeavor to maintain his Doctrine, wound the Church, delude the People, justify their Proceedings of Illusions, foment Rebellion, and call it by the Name of Liberty of Conscience.[13]

The preachers, for their part, attacked the Anglican parsons frontally, accusing them of being hireling priests and of practicing many kinds of wickedness. Their attack was not so much against persons as against the evils of the union of church and state. While their movement was still a novelty in Virginia, the Baptists dared to conceive the idea of overthrowing the establishment. The Anglicans soon learned that they were dealing with adversaries who were as daring as they were determined. Parson James Craig told Commissary Dawson that "they pray for persecution, and therefore if you fall upon any severe method of suppressing them, it will tend to strengthen their cause."[14] As a matter of fact,

---
[13] Little, *op. cit.*, pp. 233-34.
[14] Gewehr, *op. cit.*, p. 126.

persecution gave the Baptists a reputation for martyrdom which led to a popular reaction in their favor.

The persecution continued through 1774. At least thirty preachers, and perhaps more, were jailed. In some counties there was no official persecution. Imprisonments were frequent in Culpeper, Orange, Middlesex, Caroline, and Chesterfield counties, but nowhere was persecution more common than in Chesterfield. In other counties there were single cases of imprisonment.[15] The ineffectiveness of persecution in checking the growth of the sect and the outbreak of the Revolution, however, ended the imprisonments generally by 1775.

From 1770 on, local groups of Separate Baptists exercised the right of petition to gain relief from the legislature of the colony. Petitions from Baptists in Caroline, Lunenburg, Mecklenburg, and Sussex counties asked for such rights in religious matters as were accorded other dissenters.

For the first three years after the organization of the General Association of Virginia in 1771, references to politics in that body were confined to their persecutions by the government. The imprisoned preachers were considered martyrs for the truth, were prayed for at length, and were sent messages of encouragement. The Baptists had not gained sufficient strength nor had they decided upon a course of action to challenge the government prior to 1775. In that year, however, when the Association met with Dover Church, the Revolutionary controversy was reaching a climax; and they demanded action.

Messengers from sixty churches debated at length on measures to be adopted. They knew that more than a few days would be needed to prepare resolutions, addresses, and other papers, all parts of a strategy; and so the meeting adjourned for three months. Then the body met again at DuPuy's meetinghouse in Powhatan County and agreed upon a memorial addressed to the state convention, which was soon to convene. This memorial

---

[15] For example, Fauquier, Essex, and King and Queen counties are known to have imprisoned at least one preacher each.

proposed two objectives—entire independence of the Virginia colony from the mother country and complete freedom of religion in Virginia.[16]

In these far-seeing proposals the Baptists preceded all other groups in Virginia. The Presbyterians, it is true, had been petitioning the colonial legislature for two years, but their petitions were either indefinite pleas against Anglican dominance or requests for a bare religious toleration. They were cautious, fearing lest a failure of the revolutionary cause rob them of the toleration already attained.

But the Baptists boldly risked all to claim the prize of complete religious liberty. They further told the convention that they believed that, in some cases, it was lawful to go to war, that their brethren could enlist at their discretion in the colonial army, that their ministers would actively encourage the young men of the churches to enter the service, and that they desired permission for some of their ministers to serve as chaplains.

On religious freedom they spoke out plainly:

We hold that the mere toleration of religion by the civil government is not sufficient; that no State religious establishment ought to exist; that all religious denominations ought to stand upon the same footing, and that to all alike the protection of the government should be extended, guaranteeing to them the peaceful enjoyment of their religious principles, and modes of worship.[17]

Jeremiah Walker, John Williams, and George Roberts were appointed to carry the Association's messages to the convention. Upon reaching the meeting, they immediately formed an acquaintance with Thomas Jefferson, James Madison, and Patrick Henry. Henry had befriended imprisoned Baptist preachers in Chesterfield, and Madison had done the same for others in Orange. The liberal views of Jefferson on religious freedom were already well known.

---

[16] Charles F. James, *Documentary History of The Struggle for Religious Liberty in Virginia* (Lynchburg: J. P. Bell Co., 1900), pp. 51-55.

[17] Semple, *op. cit.*, p. 62.

The reading of the Baptist memorial produced "a most extraordinary and instant effect" on the convention. The body was cheered at receiving this enthusiastic offer to support the colonial cause from an entire denomination. Its reply complimented the Association's address and welcomed dissenting chaplains in the army. The Baptist messengers returned home aware that the political power represented in the General Association of Baptists was important to Virginia. In any struggle between rival parties in the state, the Baptists might well hold the balance of power.

In 1776 the example of the Baptists in addressing the legislature was followed by other denominations. Many petitions came from over the state. The Presbyterians asked for relief from taxation in order to support the church of one's choice. Churchmen and Methodists counterpetitioned to continue the establishment.

The convention, heatedly debating a course of action, continued in session from October 11 to December 5. At length it decided to tolerate dissenting religious opinions, to overlook failure to attend services of the established church, and to suspend levies supporting the clergy.[18]

The General Association sent to the 1776 legislature a paper presenting reasons for their principles earlier enunciated. Jefferson supposedly read the paper with earnest interest. At the same time, the Association sent a message of congratulation and appreciation to the newly elected Governor, Patrick Henry.

When the Association met in 1777, a committee was named to examine the laws of the Commonwealth, and single out offensive ones. Then an address was sent to the legislature, boldly asking the removal of those laws which the Baptists considered unjust. The legislature did not act directly upon this request but showed continuing sympathy with the dissenters by prolonging the suspension of church taxes.

The work of studying church-state relations became more permanent in 1778 when the General Association named a com-

[18] R. B. C. Howell, "The Influence of the Baptists on the Formation of the Virginia State Government," *The Southern Baptist Review and Eclectic*, III (1856), 463.

mittee of seven on "Civil Grievances." This committee at once reported two alarming subjects—a new scheme of taxation supporting equally all religious teachers of the leading denominations in the state and a law which would permit only Episcopal clergymen to perform weddings. Jeremiah Walker, Elijah Craig, and John Williams rushed to Richmond to present to the Assembly an address decrying these measures. Their journey was unfruitful; the Assembly was so preoccupied with the war that no effective legislation passed.

Jefferson framed and submitted to the Assembly his famous act for the establishment of religious freedom, in 1779. Jeremiah Walker brought the act before the General Association, which heartily approved it. Once more delegates were sent to the Assembly with a memorial, this one supporting Jefferson's act. Now the tide of democratic opinion was running strong, and the organized life of the established church was beginning to disintegrate. Many of the clergy declared themselves Tories and returned to England. The Assembly proceeded to repeal the support of clergy law and thus to disestablish the Church of England. Hawks, the Episcopal historian, records that "the Baptists were the principle promoters of this work, and in truth aided more than any other denomination in its accomplishment."

But the work of securing complete religious freedom only began with the disestablishment of Anglicanism. The marriage laws received fresh attention from the General Association in 1780. Largely in response to Baptist petitions, the Assembly in October made the performance of marriages lawful for any minister. All ministers, however, did not receive this privilege equally until several years later.[19]

British armies in Virginia prevented a meeting of the Association in 1781, but 1782 found that body as involved in the struggle for religious freedom as ever. The Revolutionary War ended in 1781 with political freedom, but freedom of religion did not arrive simultaneously. A fresh clamor for a tax for the support

---

[19] *Ibid.*, p. 468.

of religion was arising, and so in 1782 and 1783 the Association prepared remonstrances against this scheme. At the same time the Baptists declaimed against the glebe laws and urged passage of the bill declaring religious freedom. The government, however, was too agitated to act upon the memorials presented by Jeremiah Walker, Reuben Ford, and John Walker from the Association.

By 1783 the Separate Baptist population in Virginia exceeded ten thousand. Since delegates were scattered widely over the state, they found difficulty in attending annual associational meetings, and the Association itself was becoming unwieldy. They decided, therefore, to divide the constituency into four district associations, upper and lower districts on either side of the James River. A general committee would be set up to represent all of the districts which would act as a standing sentinel for political purposes. The General Committee of Correspondence met first in 1784 and kept up the flow of memorials to the Assembly. Remonstrances were prepared against proposed laws for a general assessment, against the Vestry Law, and against the incorporation of religious societies bill. Having laid these memorials before the legislature, Reuben Ford reported in August, 1785, that satisfactory amendments were made to the Marriage Law and that the general assessment bill was referred to popular reaction.

In the summer of 1785 the Baptists recognized a supreme crisis in their struggle. Madison had presented his "Memorial and Remonstrance Against Religious Assessments," incorporating Jefferson's Bill for Religious Freedom, which had been in the legislature mill since 1779. The people now had to decide the fate of this foundational bill. Also, there were three other vital matters before the state—the General Assessment Bill, the bill for incorporation of religious bodies, and the movement to repeal the vestry and glebe laws. The Baptists' excitement knew no bounds. Decisive leadership was needed as never before.

The General Committee drew up a Declaration of Principles, with reference to civil government, essentially "Madison's Memorial and Remonstrance." Then the Baptists sought signatures to this document from all over the state. Apparently, ten thousand citizens signed the memorial, which Reuben Ford hastily carried to the capitol.

The people of Virginia were badly divided on the four matters before their legislature. Episcopalians (Anglicans) and Methodists opposed the Baptists on all four. The Presbyterians generally favored Madison's bill establishing religious freedom, but they also favored an assessment to support religion. They were opposed to incorporating religious groups including only ministers, although they favored the incorporation of those which included the people of the churches. The Baptists stood alone among the denominations in opposing a general tax. George Washington and Patrick Henry could see nothing wrong with the assessment bill; only Jefferson and Madison took the Baptist view.[20]

In the Assembly there was a long conflict over the assessment and religious freedom bills. At length the general assessment bill was narrowly defeated. The Baptists were jubilant. Their General Committee had placed its "Declaration of Principles" into the hands of Madison, who read this document as a memorial to the legislature. This act greatly assisted passage of the law establishing religious freedom, in December, 1785.

The Baptists had won their greatest victories. However, in 1785, the legislature passed the law for incorporation of the Episcopal church, which seemed to advance the Episcopal church over other denominations. Therefore, the Baptists' General Committee in 1786 circulated petitions for repeal of the act, for selling the glebe properties, and applying the moneys to public use. Ford and John Leland were appointed to attend the circulation of the petition. The Presbyterians assisted this endeavor. The Episcopalians, however, looked upon this development as an act of vindictiveness against a church which had been reduced overnight from a position of complete superiority to near desolation. Was this not an effort on the part of the dissenting groups to destroy

---

[20] James, *op. cit.*, pp. 137-40.

the remains of the Episcopal church? Not at all said the Baptists. They wanted only to proceed consistently and thoroughly with conformity to the ideal of complete religious freedom. The official link between church and state had to be cut entirely.

The Episcopalians offered a counterpetition, but the General Assembly repealed the incorporation act in 1787. The glebe laws, however, remained. Memorials continued from the Baptists to the legislature in 1787, 1788, and afterward, but not until 1802 were the glebes actually ordered to be sold.

Meanwhile, a larger victory was being won for Virginia Baptists. The new federal Constitution was submitted to the states for ratification in 1787. The Baptists of Virginia at first rejected the Constitution since it contained no specific safeguards of religious liberty. Thus, they campaigned against ratification of the document. Then their friend James Madison persuaded them that they were following the wrong course. For the sake of the Union, the Constitution should be ratified first and afterwards it could be amended to guarantee essential liberties. He himself would labor with all his strength for such amendments. The Baptists then helped elect Madison to the Constitutional Convention of Virginia. Madison, true to his trust, led the way in transferring practically the Virginia Bill of Rights into the national Constitution as the first ten amendments. The First Amendment of that document says, "Congress shall make no law respecting an establishment of religion, or prohibiting the free exercise thereof . . ."

The unprecedented national experiment of state and church separation was underway, and no group contributed more to the establishment of that principle in American life than the Separate Baptists.

It is obvious, of course, that the common folk who composed the Baptist denomination in Virginia could not have won the struggle for freedom of religion singlehanded. The work of a small group of liberal statesmen, especially of Madison and Jefferson, was indispensable to the success of the ideal of a free church in a free state. The Baptists provided necessary popular support for the farsighted statesmen who spoke for them. Again, it must not be forgotten that other dissenting groups gave timely and significant help to the Baptists. Presbyterians and Quakers, in particular, joined the agitation for religious freedom and were important factors in securing it.

It remains true, however, that no group so consistently or so effectively campaigned for religious freedom as the Baptists. Their part in the making of what has been called America's single great contribution to the political theory of mankind—separation of church and state—cannot be easily exaggerated.

9
Claiming the Western Frontier

PRIOR TO THE REVOLUTION, Separate Baptists occupied the frontier in an almost unbroken chain from southern Virginia to Georgia. Political troubles and the pressure of population caused many to consider exploring the transmontane regions with a view to moving there, but the ruggedness of the mountains and the hostility of the redmen held them back awhile. The Regulator troubles stirred the North Carolina Separates to push westward in 1768 and afterward. Over fifteen hundred families left the Sandy Creek area following the climax of troubles at Alamance. As a rule, the migrants from south of Sandy Creek and southeastern North Carolina headed for South Carolina and Georgia. Those living north of Sandy Creek pushed westward in the direction of Tennessee. This trend continued for most of the remainder of the century.

By 1772 fully half of the Baptists of South Carolina and Georgia were in the back country, and after that date this frontier claimed a growing preponderance of the Baptist membership.[1] Nearly all of the frontier Baptists were Separates. Most of the North Carolina people who pressed westward stopped short of the mountains. A few hardy souls attempted to go beyond the North Carolina boundary to a region which they thought belonged to Virginia. Actually they went into territory presently in northeast Tennessee which had been ceded by treaty to the Cherokee Indians. In 1768 ten families from the Raleigh area began a settlement on the Watauga. Daniel Boone from the Yadkin and James

---
[1] Townsend, *op. cit.*, p. 273.

Robertson of Wake County found them there not long afterward. After the Battle of Alamance in 1771, a small party of Sandy Creek Church members settled on Boone's Creek in Washington County, Tennessee. These people were soon joined by other Separates from the Sandy Creek area. Three churches were organized, only to be broken up by the Indian war of 1774. No records of these churches have been preserved, but one of the churches is known to have had the name Buffaloe Ridge. About 1780, many of the scattered people reorganized their churches in east Tennessee.[2]

Joseph Murphy, of the Yadkin region, may have gone to Kentucky as early as 1775 to spy out the land for his people.[3] None of his people are known to have gone there immediately.[4] Probably no leaders settled permanently in Tennessee earlier than Jonathan Mulkey and Matthew Talbot. Mulkey pioneered in Carter's Valley, Hawkins County, in the fall of 1775. Talbot, also a preacher and a public man, a native of Bedford County, Virginia probably settled on the Watauga in the same year. Elder Tidence Lane may have arrived at Boone's Creek community of Watauga settlement by 1776 and is reported to have founded a church at St. Clair Bottom in 1777 or 1778.[5] He was joined by relatives and neighbors from Pittsylvania County, Virginia, by 1778. Seat[6] credits him with having led "an organized branch of Sandy Creek" to Tennessee.

Around 1780, eight Baptist preachers, including Tidence Lane and William Murphy, are said to have settled almost simultaneously in the Watauga section. With them came a Separate Baptist following, which established five or six churches by 1781.[7] In that year a conference of churches was held under Lane's leadership

---

[2] Paschal, *History*, II, 283-84.
[3] *Ibid.*, pp. 85-86.
[4] Williams, *op. cit.*, pp. 10-11.
[5] *Ibid.*, p. 11.
[6] W. R. Seat, "A History of Tennessee Baptists to 1820-25" (Doctoral dissertation, Southern Baptist Theological Seminary, 1931), p. 2.
[7] Paschal, *History*, II, 384.

and a kind of temporary association was set up. This informal body functioned as a branch of the Sandy Creek Association until it became the Holston Association in 1786. Tidence Lane was the first moderator of the Holston.

Meanwhile, during the Revolutionary period, exploration and settlement had begun in Kentucky. William Hickman, an unordained Separate Baptist preacher of Skinquarter Church, Chesterfield County, Virginia, may have been the first to preach in Kentucky. Converted by David Tinsley and baptized by Reuben Ford in 1773, he joined eight other men in laying the foundations of the Skinquarter fellowship. In time, all nine of the men became Separate Baptist ministers![8]

In the spring of 1776, Hickman and a few companions left eastern Virginia to explore the Kentucky territory. Once there, part of the company separated to go to Boonsboro, while Hickman and several others made their way to Harrodsburg. Three members of the party were preachers. Hickman and Thomas Tinsley are known to have preached in the fort at Harrodsburg. The men were attracted to the new country, but a conflict of land titles discouraged their moving immediately to Kentucky. When Hickman returned, he was ordained in 1778 and assumed the pastorate at Skinquarter. The church soon entered a series of revivals under his enthusiastic leadership.

Squire Boone of the Yadkin country, after a period of exploring with his more famous brother Daniel, moved his family from North Carolina down the Kentucky and Ohio rivers to Louisville in 1779. He had been preaching occasionally as a Separate Baptist since 1776, and so he preached in Louisville. He lived here until 1783, when he moved to Meade County, Kentucky.[9]

The zealous William Marshall of northern Virginia migrated to Kentucky in 1780, after one of his converts, John Taylor, had traversed the region and returned with glowing reports, in 1779.

[8] W. J. McGlothlin (ed.), *Publications of the Kentucky Baptist Historical Society* (Louisville: Baptist World Publishing Co., 1910), pp. 8-9.
[9] Frank M. Masters, *A History of the Baptists in Kentucky* (Louisville: Kentucky Baptist Historical Society, 1953), p. 10.

But this trickle of migrants westward during the Revolution grew to a mighty stream shortly after the close of the war. In the van marched the Separate Baptist preachers, who made natural pioneers. Persecution and adverse political conditions were but minor causes of this westward migration. Far more important was the economic pressure immediately following the Revolution. The American people had been convinced that if only the ties with England could be severed, if British interference in American affairs could be ended, an era of unparalleled prosperity must inevitably follow.

As the war drew to a successful conclusion, planters bought extensive lands and invested heavily in agricultural equipment and planting. Bumper crops resulted. But there were no markets for these goods. The West Indies, formerly America's principal market for agricultural products, were now cut off since they were British territory. English ships no longer called at American ports, and depression settled over the infant nation. Farmers were bankrupted; many lost their lands. There was but one thing for the dispossessed and the poor to do—go west where land was plentiful and offered a new beginning.

Because the Baptists were generally poor people, they felt the economic pinch most severely. Moreover, they belonged to the lower social classes. Only during the Revolution had their social status begun to rise slowly as they attracted here and there individuals of prominence and influence and as they stood in the forefront of the popular revolutionary movement. Most of the Virginia Baptists who left the East were motivated in part by dislike of the snobbery of aristocrats and large landowners. They were tired of being looked down upon as inferior. On the frontier a man could be a man, and hard work and integrity received their just reward.

Indeed, the promise of a true democracy on the frontier was the main appeal to the Baptist people. Flaming democratic idealism, denied its full expression in the class-conscious East, might have full rein in the roomy West. The frontier was a great leveler.

There one did not struggle against the restraints of ancient custom and social patterns.

Thus, while persecution had forced the early exodus of North Carolina Separate Baptists, it was economic and social factors—land hunger and the pioneering, democratic spirit—that sent Virginia Separates to the West.

With a rush the people went over the mountains. There were two principal routes to Kentucky. By far the more popular of these was that which ran through southwest Virginia and the Cumberland Gap. A host of migrants from Virginia and North Carolina pressed through the Gap to the legendary fertile lands of Kentucky. The other route, used by many Virginians and by people living north of Virginia, lay up the Potomac Valley and over the West Virginia hills to the Ohio Valley. From Wheeling and other points the migrants would float down river on various kinds of boats to the vicinity of Louisville. Thence the people would make their way inland until they found lands to their liking.

Among the earliest groups moving from Virginia were those of William Bush, of Bedford, and of Lewis Craig, of Spottsylvania. Bush had accompanied Daniel Boone in his second exploration in Kentucky. It is recorded that he assisted Boone in "blazing the trail to Boonesborough in 1775."[10] He enlisted about forty families of central Virginia in 1780 to go to the new land. Most were Separate Baptists, but whether an entire Baptist church moved is not known.

Bush preceded his company West by some months, as he hastened to Kentucky to "select and locate farms." He chose lands on the north side of the Kentucky River in present Clark County, but he encountered intense Indian hostility in that region. During the Revolution, the British had stirred the Indians to resist the westward movement of Americans. When Bush met his colonists on the Holston River, he advised them to tarry where they were until the danger of Indian hostility abated. And so the colony "raised three crops of corn" on the Holston, in present

---

[10] *Ibid.*, p. 31.

Washington County, Virginia. These people paused in their labors one day in 1781 to celebrate the news of Cornwallis' surrender in Yorktown.

Meanwhile, Lewis Craig was leading his Upper Spottsylvania Church almost in its entirety to migrate. He had been to Kentucky twice, like Joshua of old, to spy out the land in 1778 and 1780.[11] Captain William Ellis, a Revolutionary soldier, acted as military leader of the expedition which began in 1781. Lewis Craig, too, had been a regular officer in the Continental army. Four preachers in addition to Lewis Craig moved with this "traveling church." They were Joseph Craig, Elijah Craig, Ambrose Dudley, and William E. Waller. They carried a portable pulpit for their congregation of six hundred. Before them lay six hundred miles.

When the Craig people reached the Holston, they found the colony of William Bush. The ranks of the Baptists of this colony had been augmented during the pause at the Holston. An enlarged church fellowship had come into being in January, 1781, but when Lewis Craig arrived on the scene, it was decided to constitute the church. This was done on September 28, 1781, under the supervision of Lewis Craig and John Vivion. Robert Elkins, who had ministered to the group since December, 1780, became pastor.[12]

The Craig colony, more numerous, better armed, and perhaps more daring, decided to press on into Kentucky in spite of the Indian threat. Twice during their journey the colony was attacked by Indians, but losses were few. One man was killed and several cattle and horses were lost. At length the people reached their goal, Gilbert's Creek, a branch of Dix River, twenty-five miles southeast of Harrodsburg. Here the church first worshiped in their new home on the second Sunday of December, 1781. Taking the name of the creek beside the building, the Gilbert's Creek Church became the third church to appear in Kentucky.

---

[11] H. P. Hoskins, "Lewis Craig's 'Traveling Church,'" *The Chronicle*, XI (1948), 41.

[12] Masters, *op. cit.*, p. 31.

Two other Baptist churches had preceded Gilbert's Creek—Severn's Valley Church at Elizabethtown was organized June 18, 1781, and Cedar Creek Church in Nelson County, five miles southwest of Bardstown, July 4 of the same year. These churches seem to have drawn together scattered Baptists, Regular and Separate. In time they were identified as Regular Baptists, since the term "Regular" better described the Baptist mainstream on the frontier.

The Upper Spottsylvania Church, although Separate, came from the area in Virginia where Regulars were most numerous and showed an early inclination to ignore Separate and Regular distinctions. As the Gilbert's Creek Church, this body showed divided loyalties and soon experienced divisions. When Lewis Craig moved to South Elkhorn in Fayette County in 1783, most of the church apparently moved with him. Once there, he organized the South Elkhorn Church. The remnant was gathered by Joseph Bledsoe in that year on the south side of the Kentucky River and was constituted as the Gilbert's Creek Separate Baptist Church.

Meanwhile, two Baptist churches were formed in Kentucky in 1782. One of these, No-Lynn (later South Fork), was the first strictly Separate church in Kentucky. It was gathered in LaRue County by James Skaggs and Benjamin Lynn, a Pennsylvanian converted by the Separates probably in Kentucky.[13] Lynn soon left it to form the Pottenger's Creek Church. The other church organized in 1782, Forks of Dix River, in Garrard, was formed as a result of Lewis Craig's labors in its community. It was a Separate Baptist church.

The coming of several zealous and able preachers from Virginia boosted the Baptist cause so much in the years 1783-85 that it gained a primacy among the religious forces of Kentucky. One preacher was John Taylor, a convert of William Marshall. Having visited Kentucky as early as 1779, he moved there in 1783. In spite of his Separate Baptist associations, he was a

---

[13] *Ibid.,* p. 16.

Regular Baptist and held a highly Calvinistic theology. His first Kentucky revival, at Clear Creek, Woodford County, in 1784, gave rise to the Clear Creek Regular Baptist Church. His ministry was to cover the frontier from Tennessee and Kentucky to Illinois.

Even more propitious for the development of Kentucky Baptist affairs was the arrival of William Hickman in 1784. In August of the preceding year Hickman announced to his Skinquarter, Chesterfield, and Tomahawk churches that he would migrate to Kentucky a year hence. True to his word, he headed westward exactly one year to the day from the time of his announcement. His church hated to see him leave, and some members followed him for a day or two. One went with him a hundred miles.

The laborious journey took eighty-four days before the Hickman party arrived in Garrard County, Kentucky, on Saturday, November 9. On the next day Hickman preached to his family and neighbors. In April, 1785, he moved his family near Lexington, and the Hickmans joined Lewis Craig's South Elkhorn Church. From this center he carried on an itinerant ministry to surrounding areas. His reputation as a powerful preacher spread over the land. His preaching was said to have been plain and solemn, its sound "like thunder in the distance."[14]

Prominent citizens of the Forks of Elkhorn community persuaded Hickman to live among them in 1788, and they awarded him one hundred acres of land upon his arrival. Here he gathered the Forks of Elkhorn Church in 1788. However, he did not allow his pastoral responsibilities to hinder his itinerant ministry; he made missionary tours in all directions, including destitute communities. His biographer says that "the greater the destitution and the greater the danger, the more attractive to him" were the calls for service.[15] He preached much in Shelby and Scott counties and organized some twenty churches during his career. Until his death in 1830 he was the active pastor of four churches at the age

---

[14] McGlothlin, *op. cit.*, pp. 13, 17.
[15] W. P. Harvey, *A Sketch of the Life and Times of William Hickman* (Louisville: Baptist World Publishing Co., 1909), p. 14.

of eighty. "No man in Kentucky," wrote John Taylor, "baptized so many people as this venerable man."[16] During a great revival at the Forks of Elkhorn, Hickman baptized over five hundred within two years. He was called "the Gideon of the Baptist Pioneer Army in Kentucky."[17]

By the summer of 1785, eighteen Baptist churches were organized in Kentucky. Eleven of these came to be classified as Regular Baptist. It is not certain that more Regulars than Separates had gone west, but the Regulars were more careful of organization and more insistent upon a creed. Also, Baptist theology in this period decidedly tended to a consistent Calvinism. Therefore, in most congregations which drew together Regular and Separate elements, the Regular element predominated. Moreover, the preponderant alignment of the preachers in Kentucky with the Regular position had much to do with the denominational preference of their churches. By 1785 there were nineteen Regular Baptist preachers, but only eleven Separate preachers. Many who had been Separate preachers in Virginia felt no compromise in serving Regular churches in Kentucky.[18] In any case, the classification of churches into two groups was indistinct at first.

Kentucky Baptists responded to the characteristic Baptist instinct for the association of churches by 1785. In June, a conference of Baptists living north and south of the Kentucky River was held with a view to forming a general association. But since the two kinds of Baptists found their differences greater than they had supposed, no union was consummated. The group decided to meet again at Clear Creek in October. Meanwhile, five Regular churches sent delegates to a meeting of their own at South Elkhorn, on June 25, 1785. The purpose of the meeting probably was to determine the place of a confession of faith in an

---

[16] John Taylor, *History of Ten Churches* (Frankfort, Ky.: J. H. Holeman, 1823), pp. 48-49.
[17] McGlothlin, *op. cit.*, p. 24.
[18] Masters says that twenty of the first twenty-five Baptist preachers in Kentucky were Separates but that eighteen of the twenty-five soon headed Regular churches. *Op. cit.*, p. 47.

association. These churches decided upon a strict acceptance of the Philadelphia Confession, in use in the East at least as early as 1733. This decision removed all prospect of union with the Separates, who were strongly prejudiced against all confessions of faith and who disagreed with aspects of the theology of this confession in particular.

The Elkhorn Association of Regular Baptists was actually formed at Clear Creek, Woodford County, on September 30, 1785. Surprisingly, William Hickman preached the principal sermon. There was some hesitancy about labeling the group with the Regular Baptist name, but it was finally agreed that "as there are a number of Christian professors in this country under the Baptist name, in order to distinguish ourselves from them, we are of the opinion that no appelation is more suitable to our profession than that of 'Regular Baptist', which name we profess."[19]

On October 29, 1785, a second group of Regular churches, four in number, formed the Salem Association. These churches lay to the west of the Elkhorn churches.

At length, the first Separate Association appeared in October, 1787. Comprised of churches south of the Kentucky River, this body took the name South Kentucky Association of Separate Baptists. Eleven churches sent delegates to the Tate's Creek meetinghouse, and they "constituted an association on the Bible," that is acknowledging no creedal or confessional basis but the Bible. Thus, this association had one more church than the Elkhorn Association in 1787, and five more than the Salem Association. Its member churches were Boone's Creek, Fayette County (Joseph Craig, pastor); Forks of Dix River, Garrard County (Joseph Bledsoe, pastor); Head of Boone's Creek, Fayette County (Joseph Craig, pastor); Huston's Creek, Bourbon County (Moses Bledsoe, pastor); Lick Creek, Nelson County (Benjamin Lynn, pastor); Nolin, LaRue County (Joseph Skaggs, pastor); Providence, Clark County (Robert Elkin, pastor); Rush Branch, Lincoln County

---

[19] *Ibid.*, p. 53.

(John Bailey, pastor); and Tate's Creek, Madison County (Andrew Tribble, pastor).[20]

Churches of this association continued a number of primitive rites which had been identified with the Separate movement earlier in North Carolina and Virginia. The ordinance of footwashing was kept at least to the end of the century. These churches tended also to concentrate more authority in the hands of its ministers than was usual among Regular Baptists. Beyond this, they showed a conservatism which would hinder their progress and a lack of doctrinal stability which would later invite doctrinal innovations and militate against the unity of the churches.

The Separate Baptist migration became a flood between 1785 and 1815. The pioneering fever claimed entire communities in all parts of Virginia and North Carolina. Fully a third of the Separate Baptist constituency in Virginia went to Kentucky. Well over a third of the preachers went with the people. Even old and long established preachers were caught up by the enthusiasm and headed west. Kentucky was spoken of as "the graveyard of Virginia Baptist preachers."

The Baptists were fitted for life on the frontier, for they made ideal western pioneers. Being hardworking yeomen, they were equal to the herculean physical tasks necessary in the frontier wilderness. They were not afraid of hard work. Also, their ideas of freedom and democracy were suited for the new region, where wealth and social prestige did not separate neighbors. Unused to money earlier, they were soon at home in the new money-scarce economy.

Moreover, the church polity of the Baptists was adapted to frontier conditions. Organizing a Baptist church in a frontier community was a simple task. Unlike the methodology of Shubal Stearns and his cohorts, it was done without consulting anyone beyond the little band of migrants who had discovered a sense of fellowship and wished to become a church. The people were drawn together by the Word and the Spirit of God. It mattered

---

[20] *Ibid.*, pp. 63-64.

not whether this occurred on the road or in a cabin in the wilderness. There was no need to wait for a bishop, a presiding elder, or a presbytery to set things in order. The congregation simply chose one member who could write to act as clerk, several who had gifts of leadership to be deacons, and one or more who could exhort to be preachers.

A preacher was designated as minister, although he was almost always without formal training for his pastoral office. The minister was one of his people, working with them in the forests or the fields for six days of the week and preaching on Sunday. He was free at some seasons to leave his manual labor and go on preaching tours in response to calls for a ministry to scattered settlements. He thus itinerated widely and, in a measure, kept pace with the far-ranging Methodist circuit rider system, which provided so valuable a service to the frontier. But, unlike the circuit rider, the Baptist farmer-preacher always was closely identified with a particular home base and a local community of God's children. He did not earn his living by preaching, although his people shared with him some of the fruits of their labors. He was the person of greatest honor in the disciplined communities served by him, but he was always one of the people.

The Separate Baptists grew with the frontier, fitting in with its conservative but nonconformist character. In the merging Baptist traditions they found their places in both Separate and Regular Baptist churches. Their greatest achievement was in their riding the crest of the westward migration all along the southern frontier. They were heroic witnesses for Christ in a most strategic era and place in American history.

10
Post-Revolutionary Revival and Merger

THE AMERICAN REVOLUTION appeared to put an end to the Separate Baptist revival. From the outbreak of war and for some years after its conclusion, the Baptist movement showed a marked decline in growth. It was not an abatement of zeal, however, as much as several other factors, which caused this decline. Among these factors were preoccupation with the Revolution, the westward migration, and an enlarged commercialism. Perhaps more important than any of these was the rise of another aggressive revival movement—Methodism. The Methodist phase of the Great Awakening in the South began at the start of the Revolutionary War and continued until its end. Methodism, finding its greatest success in Virginia, largely wrested religious leadership from the Baptists in the south-central, and the southeastern parts of the state. In other areas it challenged and, in many cases, checked Baptist growth.

It may well be true that Methodism disturbed the Separate Baptists more internally than externally. A few of their outstanding leaders were strongly attracted to its Arminian theology, and this subject became a serious divisive issue for a time. The honored John Waller fell under the influence of a Methodist preacher Robert Williams and fully embraced Arminian doctrine in 1775 or 1776, although he remained a Baptist. At the meeting of the General Association in 1776, he tried to propound his new views. When he failed to convince the Association, he withdrew from it, carrying a number of followers with him. He and his adherents then embarked upon a widespread, independent work, often in competition with the associated churches. They itinerated widely, raised up a company of lay elders, whom Waller ordained, and gathered great multitudes for novel camp meetings. This defection from the Separates continued until 1787.[1]

Jeremiah Walker, who had helped plant twenty to thirty churches south of the James River, also became an ardent Arminian. Imprisoned with David Tinsley for unlicensed preaching, he converted Tinsley to Arminian views while in Chesterfield County jail. Moving to Georgia soon after, he quickly won a following. When he was unable to convince the Georgia Association of his views, he led in forming a new Baptist association on Arminian principles. Walker made several trips back to Virginia. On one trip he was accompanied by Silas Mercer, of Georgia, a convincing Calvinist. Mercer more than neutralized the effect of Walker's doctrinal preaching, both before the churches and the General Committee.[2] After 1790, the Virginia Separates inclined more uniformly to Calvinistic views.

The war period, however, must not be thought of as a time of stagnation or decline among the Separates. Ryland[3] records that thirty-seven new churches were organized during the Revolution in twenty-eight different Virginia counties. In thirteen of these counties there had been no Baptist church before. Elijah Baker had phenomenal success planting churches on the Eastern Shore of Virginia. There was, likewise, satisfactory growth in parts of North Carolina not directly affected by military operations.

At the same time, from 1775 until 1785 reports of "coldness and dissention" came repeatedly from the churches. It appeared to many that the Baptist enthusiasm had spent itself and would not reappear. Those who held this view soon saw their error.

Some men, like Silas Mercer in North Carolina, engaged in ceaseless itineracy throughout the war period. From his base in Halifax, North Carolina, Mercer went forth to preach at least once a day for six years. He showed the same zeal in Georgia after the

---

[1] Taylor, *Virginia Baptist Ministers*, pp. 81-82.
[2] Semple, *op. cit.*, pp. 81-83.
[3] *Op. cit.*, p. 114.

war.[4] The Grassy Creek community in North Carolina saw a great awakening in 1775. In Georgia, Daniel Marshall was the only minister of any denomination to remain at his post through the war, after which he led his people in extensive revivals and rapid growth.[5] Revival reached the South Carolina churches at Charleston and Welsh Neck in 1785 and 1790, respectively.[6]

The forerunner of a new awakening in Virginia, John Leland, came from Massachusetts to Virginia in 1777. From his base in Culpeper County, he itinerated as far south as the Pee Dee in South Carolina. Then, moving from Culpeper to Orange County, Leland began to concentrate his efforts upon Virginia counties east of Orange in 1779. His first significant successes were in York County. He baptized 130 converts from November, 1779 to July, 1780. Then followed a "slack time religiously," according to Leland, although he continued to itinerate, touring northward to Philadelphia and southward into North Carolina.

Leland's greatest revivals lay yet ahead. On a six-week tour of the middle counties of North Carolina in 1785, he gathered an abundant harvest.[7] Then in August, 1786, he visited the venerable Samuel Harris in Pittsylvania and joined him on a tour through Orange, Fluvanna, Louisa, and Goochland counties. Their preaching awakened many.

In 1785 there was an awakening under Separate Baptist preaching all along the James River Valley in Virginia. It continued with some interruptions until 1792.[8] Leland baptized three hundred people in 1788. Before he returned to live in Massachusetts in 1792, he had baptized seven hundred and had given valuable leadership in the Baptists' campaign for full religious freedom. His most effective revival occurred in a twenty-mile-square area around his residence in Orange. Samuel Harris, apparently,

---

[4] B. D. Ragsdale, *The Story of Georgia Baptists* (Atlanta: Executive Committee, Georgia Baptist Convention, 1938), pp. 12-13.
[5] *Ibid.*, p. 11.
[6] Townsend, *op. cit.*, p. 76.
[7] Taylor, *Virginia Baptist Ministers*, p. 34.
[8] Semple, *op. cit.*, pp. 36, 38.

triggered this awakening by a visit late in 1787, when revival broke out "like a mighty torrent."[9] "Frivolity" fled the entire countryside.

The revival which began at the James River spread northward into the eastern midland and the northern parts of Virginia, culminating in 1787-89. The Dover, Goshen, and Culpeper associations were greatly stirred. Churches in the Northern Neck and Caroline and King and Queen counties, to the east, were quickened and enlarged. In the Middle District Association the period 1787-91 was "a time of ingathering of souls."[10] Northward, the revival swept over Fairfax and Stafford counties and westward to the Blue Ridge.

The Ketoctan Regular Baptist Association partook of the fervor and began to send its preachers on evangelizing tours. Indeed, the Regular preachers were the leading figures in the revival in the Northern Neck and in northern Virginia. Youthful Lewis Lunsford traveled day and night on preaching tours to the Valley and the Northern Neck. Three of his journeys reached Kentucky. Jeremiah Moore claimed that he had traveled far enough on preaching tours to have circled the globe twice. He ranged from the Carolinas to Pennsylvania and from Maryland to Tennessee.[11]

This revival checked the spread of Methodism in most of Virginia, and it consolidated the position of the Baptists as the largest Christian body in the state.

Some features of the post-Revolutionary revivalism are noteworthy. Physical and emotional manifestations again appeared in the revival meetings of 1785-92. It was not uncommon in meetings to see a large portion of a congregation writhing in anguish upon the floor. In the larger meetings, several ministers would be preaching at the same time in different parts of the building. The noise was great; confusion, if not disorder, often was evident.

---

[9] L. F. Greene (ed.), *The Writings of the Late Elder John Leland* (New York, 1845), p. 26.

[10] L. W. Moore, *A History of the Middle District Association* (Richmond: Virginia Baptist Historical Society, 1886), p. 23.

[11] Gewehr, *op. cit.*, p. 118.

Post-Revolutionary Revival and Merger 137

A reaction against emotional and physical extravagances arose, however, and men began to speak of the dangers of hypocrisy in certain of these displays of feeling. Some of the manifestations quickly fell into disfavor.

Thus the manner of preaching became more orderly. In large measure, this could be accounted for by the rising social status of the Baptists. The most respectable and prominent citizens of many communities were now identifying themselves with Baptist churches. They were no longer chiefly churches of the poor and underprivileged. This social revolution reflected in their fading interest in puritanical simplicity and plainness of dress. "Scrupulosity about little matters was laid aside."[12]

Music played a larger part in this revival than in the earlier ones. People went singing to meetings, sang more during the services, and sang on their way home. New vernacular hymns appeared; many were set to popular tunes previously nonreligious.

Semple notes that the post-Revolutionary phase of the Separate Baptist revivalism differed from the earlier phase in that it did not produce many young preachers. John Leland attributes this failure to three factors which are indeed sufficient explanation. First, the old preachers stood in the way, assuming posts of leadership which earlier had been available to young men. Second, there was too little prayer for laborers. Third, the judgment of God rested upon the people for their failure to support the ministry.[13] The old Separate Baptist prejudice against a paid ministry lived on, and so the quality of the ministry began to suffer. Further, the promise of economic opportunity was drawing many young men to the frontier.

Doctrinally, the period witnessed a strengthening of Calvinism among Separate Baptists. A tendency toward speculative thought, to which Separates had so long been averse, now appeared among the preachers. The pressure of Methodist Arminianism drove some to antinomianism and relaxation of church discipline. Some

---
[12] Semple, *op. cit.*, p. 39.
[13] *Ibid.*, p. 38.

who spoke dogmatically about their own election failed to give due importance to consistent Christian living. This was the saddest aspect of an otherwise exciting and optimistic era.

Possibly the most beneficial result of the post-Revolutionary revivals in various parts of the South was the uniting of Separate and Regular Baptists. Other factors, of course, aided this union, but nothing drew the two kinds of Baptists together into a common community so much as the revival spirit. It was their interest in evangelism which gradually erased their differences.

After the Virginia Separate Association rebuffed the overtures of union made by the Ketocton Regular Association in 1770, the Philadelphia Association began to promote the idea of joining the Separate churches. Philadelphia messengers were sent to visit these churches, and an exchange of associational minutes among all Baptist groups was encouraged. Morgan Edwards visited the Congaree Separate Association in South Carolina in 1772 and was able to persuade that body to correspond annually with the Philadelphia Association.

The South Carolina Separates were even willing to explore the possibility of co-operating with the Charleston Regular Association, their neighbors to the east. Marshall, Reese, and Newman, "commissioners appointed by a general meeting of the Separates held at the Congaree" in 1773, were sent to discuss a union with the Charleston Association at its meeting. The Regulars found these Separates to be "tenacious of their peculiarities," and so nothing came of the discussions. The Charleston people felt that the Separates were too distinctive and that they tended to Arminianism. Again in 1775, Philip Mulkey appeared in Charleston with a proposal from the Congaree that "the several associations in this Province" unite. This, too, was killed by the suspicious Charleston Association.[14]

In 1776 the Congaree Association developed internal difficulties by attempting to exercise too much control over member churches. Dissension among the churches and the dislocations of the Revolu-

---

[14] Townsend, *op. cit.*, pp. 174-75.

Post-Revolutionary Revival and Merger 139

tion led to the break up of the Congaree soon after. The union of Baptists in South Carolina had to await the conclusion of the Revolution.

In North Carolina, the Kehukee Association, already infiltrated by Separate influences, sent delegates to the Virginia Separate Association in 1772. The Virginia Separates agreed to their request in sending two ministers to the Kehukee meeting in 1772 to explore possibilities of a union. The Separate delegates vetoed the proposed union on the basis of three objections: first, the Regulars were not properly strict in receiving members; second, they indulged in superfluity of dress; and, third, the Regulars retained members who had been baptized in unbelief. This last objection was most serious. It concerned former General Baptists who admitted that they had not been converted prior to baptism and yet were not rebaptized when they became Regulars.[15]

These objections were taken so seriously by some Kehukee churches that they declared disfellowship with members who confessed that they had been baptized in unbelief. Other churches objected to this procedure, and the Kehukee was split in 1775. The reformed churches made a new beginning in 1777, organizing a new association which included four Separate churches as well as six Regular ones. This was the first association to include both Regular and Separate churches. A Calvinistic "Abstract of Principles" was published by the new association.

The common interest in the struggle for complete religious freedom helped unite Separate and Regular Baptists in Virginia. In the midst of that contest, the Separates took a step which removed a primary obstacle to the union when they adopted the Philadelphia Confession of Faith. Circumstances leading to this conclusion are worthy of review. The General Association's unwieldiness had resulted in its division into districts. The fourfold division agreed upon in 1776 had not been thoroughly worked out as late as 1783, when a decision was finally effected to divide churches north of the James into upper and lower districts. At

---

[15] Semple, *op. cit.*, p. 349.

that time, John Williams, former sheriff of Lunenburg County, pastor of the large Meherrin Church, and a leading spirit in the Association, moved the adoption of the Philadelphia confession as a standard of principles. He mentioned the appropriateness of doing so before the churches divided into two sections.

The Association agreed to adopt the confession, with the following proviso:

> To prevent its usurping a tyrannical power over the consciences of any, we do not mean that every person is to be bound to the strict observance of everything therein contained, nor do we mean to make it, in any respect, superior or equal to the scriptures in matters of faith and practice; although we think it the best human composition of the kind now extant; yet it shall be liable to alteration whenever the General Committee, in behalf of the associations, shall think fit.[16]

Especially for the purpose of carrying to its logical conclusion the principle of separation of church and state, the district associations created a General Committee. It replaced the General Association of Separate Baptists. As the committee's organizational meeting in October, 1784, representatives of the Ketocton Regular Association were admitted on the same basis as other district associations. Together the representatives of the two Baptist groups pressed the fight against religious discrimination in Virginia.

Since their leaders had joined to fight for liberty and the people had shared a common faith and revival, the Baptists felt impelled to seek union with one another. Therefore, the General Committee recommended to the several associations of Virginia that they send delegates to the Committee's 1787 meeting to effect the desired union. When the delegates assembled, the Philadelphia Confession, as received by the General Association in 1783, was recommended to them. Some opposed the adoption of any confession, but it was finally passed with the following statement:

> To prevent the confession of faith from usurping a tyrannical power over the conscience of any, we do not mean, that every person is

---

[16] *Ibid.*, p. 68.

Post-Revolutionary Revival and Merger 141

bound to the strict observance of everything therein contained; yet that it holds forth the essential truths of the gospel, and that the doctrine of salvation by Christ and free unmerited grace alone, ought to be believed by every Christian and maintained by every minister of the gospel. Upon these terms we are united; and desire hereafter that the names Regular and Separate, be buried in oblivion; and that, from hence forth, we shall be known by the name of the United Baptist Churches of Christ in Virginia.[17]

Even John Waller's "Independents" joined in the happy union. Waller had tired of separation from his brethren in spite of his wonderful success, and he was already partially restored to fellowship. The restoration of Waller and his followers was made official in 1787.[18]

John Leland had been ordained without the imposition of hands. Since he wished to aid the spirit of brotherhood, he freely submitted to the rite at the hands of a presbytery.[19] Everyone wanted to please his brother in this time of rejoicing and good feeling.

Revivals were widespread at the time of the union. A great outbreak of the revival spirit occurred in 1787 in north central Virginia under the preaching of John Waller. Hundreds were baptized as a result of his meetings, which lasted with little interruption through 1792. Passing his mantle to his nephew Andrew Waller, the old preacher migrated to South Carolina in 1793. John Leland baptized hundreds in 1787 and 1788. Upper King and Queen Church had an unprecedented awakening beginning in 1788. Nomini Church in the Northern Neck and Tuckahoe Church in Caroline baptized three hundred members each in revival seasons at this time. And the Ketocton Association awakening reached its climax in 1789, when three hundred and fifty were baptized. Seven years earlier only twenty-three baptisms had been reported in this association during twelve months.[20]

The bulky name agreed upon for the combined Baptist forces

---
[17] *Ibid.*, pp. 73-75.
[18] Taylor, *Virginia Baptist Ministers*, p. 82.
[19] Greene, *op. cit.*, p. 26.
[20] Masters, *op. cit.*, p. 48.

was soon shortened in common usage to "United Baptists." Then in a few years, the "United" was dropped. The Virginia union proved the most influential of Baptist unions throughout the country. And it was the largest, since the Baptist population in Virginia outnumbered that of any other state.

Regular and Separate Baptists beyond Virginia, except in Kentucky, quickly combined forces. In North Carolina a small union was effected among Baptists in the eastern part of the state in 1788. War had kept the reformed Kehukee Regular Association (now the United Baptist Association and led by Lemuel Burkitt) from uniting with the Separates after 1777. In 1785, however, the Association again appointed a committee to work out a plan to combine all Regulars and Separates. This committee reported in May, 1786, recommending the following terms of union:

1. We think that none but believers in Christ have a right to the ordinance of baptism; therefore, we will not hold communion with those who plead for the validity of baptism in unbelief.
2. We leave every church member to decide for himself whether he has been baptized in unbelief or not.
3. We leave every minister at liberty to baptize, or not, such persons as desire to be baptized, being scrupulous about their former baptism.[21]

The Association agreed to these terms, and its churches ratified them. At its 1788 session, the churches at Newport and New River, two of the leading Separate churches of the region, sought admission to the Association and were received. At that time the following resolution was passed:

That those bars which heretofore subsisted between the Baptists amongst us, formerly called Regulars and Separates, be taken down; and that a general union and communion take place according to the terms proposed at brother Joshua Freeman's in Bertie County, May, 1786; and that the names Regular and Separate be buried in oblivion, and that we should henceforth be known to the world by the name United Baptist.[22]

---
[21] Paschal, *History*, I, 492-93.
[22] *Ibid.*, p. 493.

Some of the Separate churches of eastern North Carolina now began to join the United Association. In other parts of the state, official action uniting the two kinds of Baptists was not taken. The Yadkin Association, for example, took no notice of distinctions at its organization in 1787, but it contained Regulars and Separates. The two movements quietly coalesced at the level of the district association.

South Carolina and Georgia Baptists began interassociational correspondence after the Revolution, and churches were received into associations without regard for their Separate or Regular traditions. Fusion took place without formal acts of union.

In Tennessee, the Holston Association churches from the beginning apparently included both Separate and Regular Baptists. The Separates predominated but approximated the Regulars' theology. Holston was willing to adopt the Philadelphia confession as a basis of union but "only as a general system of principles." Detailed allegiance to the confession was not demanded.[23]

As soon as union had been consummated in Virginia, the Virginians began to urge their Kentucky brethren to work for a similar union. Messages to this effect were received in Kentucky before the end of 1787.[24] A Baptist Committee in Richmond addressed a letter on this subject, dated October 2, 1788, to the South Kentucky Association. The Kentucky body thought it was placed in fellowship with the United Baptists of Virginia, but they did not consider their entering this fellowship as binding them to receive "any part of the Philadelphia Confession of Faith." These Separates agreed to assume the name "United Baptist Association in Kentucky."[25]

At the May, 1789, meeting of the Elkhorn Association, the Great Crossings Church presented a letter from the Virginia

---

[23] Seat, *op. cit.*, p. 32. It is interesting to note that Tidence Lane bequeathed two books to his son Acquilla, one of which was the "Baptist Confession of Faith." Burnett, *Sketches of Tennessee's Pioneer Baptist Preachers*, p. 556.
[24] Masters, *op. cit.*, p. 48.
[25] *Ibid.*, pp. 55, 66.

General Committee recommending a union of Baptist forces in Kentucky. The Elkhorn responded by agreeing to drop the name Regular from all letters of the association. At the same time, the Elkhorn received a request from the South Kentucky to discuss the union of the two associations.

A joint committee met in August, 1789, at Harrod's meetinghouse, but it failed. The parties still regarded each other with suspicion. The Regulars thought the Separates were unsound in their indefinite, undogmatic attitude toward doctrines and their practice of open communion. And the Separates were still unable to overcome their prejudice against confessions of faith.

But the matter of union would not die. The Elkhorn sent messengers to the Tate's Creek meeting of the South Kentucky Association, desiring union, in June, 1793. It was agreed to call a convention of delegates from the churches at Marble Creek Church, Fayette County, in July. The Philadelphia Confession proved once more the bone of contention, and hopes for union were dashed. However, South Kentucky was willing at its meeting the following October to study certain terms of union proposed by the Regulars. Upon rejection of these terms, five ministers and four churches withdrew from the South Kentucky Association. The four churches—Head of Boone's Creek, Jessamine, Forks of Dix River, and Hickman's Creek—formed an association afterwards called Tate's Creek.[26]

The Tate's Creek Association, formed in 1793, took the name United Baptists and sent a member Thomas Shelton to bear the associational letter to the General Committee of Virginia. Shelton was killed by Indians on his way to Virginia. A correspondence was also begun with the Elkhorn Association in 1793 but suspended thereafter until 1797.[27]

The stalemate in Kentucky was at last broken by the great revival which swept the frontier, 1800 to 1803. Beginning among Virginia Presbyterians and reaching the frontier with the preaching

[26] *Ibid.*, p. 65.
[27] *Ibid.*, p. 57.

Post-Revolutionary Revival and Merger 145

of the Presbyterian James McGready, this awakening quickly evangelized the entire frontier region and delivered it from the threat of lawlessness and barbarism. The masses were reached by means of camp meetings, which became abiding features of frontier religious life. Thousands of scattered folk traveled many miles to attend these meetings. Once on the camp grounds, they pitched tents or other shelters and spent days or weeks hearing the gospel.

Methodists and Baptists joined heartily with the Presbyterians in the preaching. Often half a dozen preachers would be proclaiming their faith at once in different corners of the forest clearing. All of the participating denominations grew rapidly as a result of the revival. Kentucky Baptist churches added some ten thousand members in three years. Great excitement abounded in the region, and many physical and emotional manifestations attracted much attention. The people displayed dancing, falling, barking, shouting, jerking, fainting, trances, and visions.

On the whole, Baptists and Presbyterians discouraged these exhibitions. Neither would the Baptists join the others in their open communion services. When time came for observance of the Lord's Supper at the camp meetings, the Baptists would retire to limit the ordinance to believers baptized upon profession of their faith. Thus Separate and Regular Baptists were thrown together, sharing alike the Lord's table and the revival enthusiasm. They realized that they were in fact one people.

The Elkhorn Association led in appointing a committee in 1800 to visit the South Kentucky on calling a convention. The South Kentucky then named a committee to confer with the Regulars, and the joint committee drew up new terms of union. These terms were approved by the Separates. Then a convention was held at Old Providence meetinghouse on Howard's Creek, Clark County, on the second Saturday in October, 1801. Messengers from the churches, two from each church, approved the following union, before asking the churches for formal adoption:

We the committee of Elkhorn and South Kentucky Associations, do agree to unite on the following plan:

1. That the Scriptures of the Old and New Testaments are the infallible Word of God, and the only rule of faith and practice.
2. That there is one only true God, and in the Godhead, or divine essence, there are Father, Son, and Holy Ghost.
3. That by nature we are fallen and depraved creatures.
4. That Salvation, regeneration, sanctification, and justification are by the life, death, resurrection and ascension of Jesus Christ.
5. That the saints will finally persevere through grace to glory.
6. That Believers' baptism by immersion is necessary to receiving the Lord's Supper.
7. That the salvation of the righteous and punishment of the wicked will be eternal.
8. That it is our duty to be tender and affectionate to each other, and study the happiness of the children of God in general; and to be engaged singly to promote the honor of God.
9. And that the preaching (that) Christ tasted death for every man, shall be no bar to communion.
10. And that each may keep their associational and church government as to them seem best.
11. That a free correspondence and communion be kept between the churches thus united.

Unanimously agreed to by the joint committee:

Ambrose Dudley	Robert Elkin
John Price	Thomas J. Chilton
Joseph Redding	Daniel Ramey
David Barrow	Moses Bledsoe
	Samuel Johnson[28]

The new fellowship took the name "General Union of Separate and Regular Baptists." This was afterward shortened to "United Baptists," a name which continued long in Kentucky. Only two associations actually were united by the merger of 1801, but other Kentucky associations rejoiced in the union movement and identified themselves with the United Baptist name. Baptists of the entire frontier were soon united in fellowship, for the influence of the Kentucky associations was far-reaching. By 1801 the Elkhorn alone claimed thirty-seven churches from the mouth of the Little Miami, Ohio to the Cumberland settlement in Tennessee.

---

[28] *Ibid.,* pp. 158-59.

11
Significance of the Movement

THE SEPARATE BAPTIST MOVEMENT in the South was undoubtedly one of the most formative influences ever brought to bear upon American religious life. Its part in the shaping of religious ideals and patterns among the American people has been realized by few scholars and has been almost entirely ignored by laymen. Because the name Separate Baptist fell into disuse, its distinctive contributions also were forgotten.

As revivers of the Great Awakening in the South, the Separate Baptists merit special attention. In this role they were anticipated by the Presbyterians in Virginia, who, however, led a revival movement of very limited duration and scope. Hampered by lofty ministerial standards and a rigid confessionalism, the Presbyterian revival failed to reach the masses of the Southern Colonies. Also, a climate of readiness for revival was lacking during the time of Presbyterian leadership.

But the Separate Baptists appeared in the fullness of the times. Men had grown conscious of their religious needs. They only needed messengers who could speak understandably to those needs. Social and political conditions were ripe for a great popular response to the teachings of an indigenous ministry. Religiously, the new land was unoccupied; the minds and hearts of the people were ready to be claimed by apostles of a vital Christian message.

The Baptist preachers knew the language of the common man. Uninhibited by the lack of a formal education, they were able to supply the people's demands of thought and emotion. In the brief span of twenty years they spearheaded an unprecedentedly popular religious movement, and within thirty years their people established themselves as the leading denomination of the South. Popular enthusiasm for the movement matched that of the greatest revivals in Christian history. In this respect, the Separate Baptist movement has been compared with the Puritan movement of seventeenth-century England, with Lollardy of the fourteenth century, and with the Barefoot Friars of the thirteenth.[1]

As popularizers of revivalism in the South, the Baptists opened the way for a resourceful Methodism and helped establish the character of American evangelical Christianity. Their awakening marked the beginning of an aggressive Christianity in their region. More than any other group, they impressed the revivalistic stamp upon American religious life. It is agreed that "revivalism has proved to be as distinctive of American Protestantism as it has been characteristic."[2] Other features of American Christianity, including its "strongly biblical, individualistic, parochial, and practical" character, have remained fixed since the Great Awakening.[3] The Baptist contributions fall particularly under the heads of voluntaryism, democracy, and denominationalism. The Separate awakening insured the permanence of these elements and of an interpretation of Christianity which was solidly based upon the Bible.

The significance of the Separate Baptist movement is further indicated in the fact that it largely provided religious leadership for the American frontier. There liberty always threatened to degenerate into license, and the law of the wilderness dared to become the law of the land. But among the scattered settlements moved preachers and people who urged and practiced obedience to the law within. In the fight for survival on the dangerous frontier, men derived sense and direction for their struggle from religious revival. The Separate Baptist preachers preceded most others in exploring and occupying the frontier. They were already

---

[1] Mosteller, "Separate Baptists," p. 154.
[2] Peter G. Mode, *The Frontier Spirit in American Christianity* (New York: Macmillan Co., 1923), p. 45.
[3] Nichols, *op. cit.*, p. 186.

Significance of the Movement 149

there when most of the settlers came. The people responded to their leadership and gave them due honor. When the pioneer spirit would not die and the people pushed on west, the pastors went with them. The frontier could not be ignored.

Again, the moral and spiritual preparation which the Separate revival made in the struggle for American liberty cannot be easily exaggerated. No people stood more united for the revolutionary cause than the Separate Baptists, and none was so zealous as they in the contest for religious liberty. Their espousal of democracy and free-church ideals placed them in the forefront of the revolutionary movement. Thus they were able to provide much of the spiritual inspiration needed for the arduous tasks of the Revolution. On the other hand, the social situation of which they were a part reinforced the distinctive teaching of their revival—religious individualism. The frontiersman was a rugged individualist, and the Baptist emphasis agreed entirely with his individualism. In the Revolution, Baptist and Presbyterian meetinghouses were regularly burned by the British as nests of rebellion. Baptist and Presbyterian pastors were hunted as leaders of insurrection.

The success of the Revolution naturally saw the triumph of free-church principles in government and in religion. The "Radical Reformation" thus triumphed in America as nowhere else in the entire world. Its concept of the church as a voluntary fellowship of deliberate followers of Christ came to prevail in the Southern region and in other parts of the country.

The appeal of Separate revivalism was felt strongly among the Negro people of the South. Before the Baptists arrived, the Presbyterians already had some success in evangelizing the slaves. However, this success was confined to a small area of Virginia. The Separate Baptists were able to reach the Negro better than any before them. Earliest Baptist churches received Negro members on the same terms as white members. Some had more Negroes than white. Thus was initiated the marvelous work of evangelizing the Negro race in the South, which resulted in a preponderant alignment of Negro people with the Baptists in America.

The success of the Separate Baptist movement rested upon sure foundations. The Separates presented the doctrine of the Awakening in such fashion as to appeal most strongly to the masses. An indigenous ministry and widespread use of lay preaching were prime ingredients in this appeal. Their individualizing of religion meant their emotionalizing of religion.[4] Addressing the emotions and the mind proved far more effective than addressing the mind alone. Fundamental evangelical doctrines took hold of the popular mind more forcefully than lectures on morality and duty.

This primary formula for Baptist success was aided by the social factor of dislike for the ruling class and the economic factor of double taxation. Also, politically the times favored the Baptists. The incoming tide of freedom and democracy made them immediately popular as valiant exponents of the cause of the people.[5]

The Separate Baptist movement, however, was not without weaknesses. Among these were too great dependence upon mass evangelism and excessive emotional appeal. Parodoxically, the Separate Baptist preachers showed marked respect for personality in trying to bring men to individual repentance and faith, but, at the same time, they used mass psychology almost exclusively to effect a decision.[6] In view of the emotional starvation in the religion of the southern people, it was inevitable that the enthusiastic Separates should appeal to the emotions. Occasionally, this appeal became an end in itself or got out of hand. Some of the visions, trances, and hallucinations of revivalism probably resulted from self-hypnotism. The intellectual content of the message was thus obscured.

Other weaknesses involved the ministry. Ministerial education was definitely undervalued. Grounds for this attitude must be

---

[4] W. W. Sweet, *Revivalism in America*, p. 26.

[5] Gewehr, *op. cit.*, pp. 136-37.

[6] D. W. Armstrong, "An Examination of American Evangelism Beginning with the 18th Century in the Light of N. T. Principles of Evangelism" (Doctoral dissertation, Southern Baptist Theological Seminary, 1955), p. 96.

sought, during the Revolutionary era, in the popular dislike of the established church, whose ministry often emphasized education almost to the exclusion of personal piety.

However, this attitude of the Separates rested more decidedly upon their own ideas of Christian illumination and vocation. The individual's experience of radical conversion was so fundamental to their thinking that supplementary equipment and training for witnessing were counted of little significance. Moreover, the immediate guidance of the Holy Spirit was reckoned the single necessary equipment for doing God's bidding. The Spirit would certainly aid those ministers whom he should call and commission. Education was counted insignificant as compared with charismatic endowment. The two were not mutually exclusive, but in the existential situation of mystical experience and religious challenge, it seemed obvious that the nonessential would be passed by and the essential regarded. There was, in fact, scarcely a minister in the Separate Baptist ministry who had had formal schooling for his ministry.

Practical substantiation of the Separates' view regarding ministerial education was found in the amazing growth of their movement while the established church declined. Charismatic ability proved far more effective than theological training in the schools.

The preachers' lack of education gave them a decided advantage during early stages of their movement. It placed them on the same plane as the people to whom they ministered and established a bond of sympathy between them and their hearers. Later, however, the Separate Baptists recognized the lack of ministerial education as a real handicap to progress. They began to propose schools for ministers toward the close of the eighteenth century, although they were not successful in founding such schools until after the first quarter of the nineteenth.

The Separates' neglect of ministerial education was paralleled by their failure to give most of their people more than a rudimentary education in the Christian faith and worship. The Separates did not try to educate men so much as to "alarm" them. Once men were awakened, they reasoned, they would be taught by the Holy Spirit.

Nonpayment of the ministry by the Separates was a novelty, which early in the movement attracted attention and gained considerable approbation for the preachers. Many people, associating church taxes and mercenary motives with the Anglican ministry, credited the Baptist preachers with a superior spirituality when they refused pay. Stearns and his fellows rejoiced to preach the gospel without charge to the poor. Their successors usually rejected salaries from their churches, although voluntary offerings were received at times.[7]

Among the preachers there developed a pride over their independence from formal church support and their resulting poverty. Brother Soelle, the Moravian minister, recorded in his diary in 1773 that "it is the method and plan of the Baptists to give their preachers nothing, and they must support themselves by the work of their hands."[8] Some years after his ministry began in Virginia, William Hickman was given twelve dollars for conducting the funeral of an Episcopalian lady. He said that this was the first cash he had ever received as a "money preacher," and he was reluctant to accept it.[9] Especially among the Separates of Virginia, the motto "A Free Church and a Free Gospel" was heard. A "Free Gospel" usually included neglect of ministerial support. Unwittingly, the preachers taught their people unscriptural views on the subject.

In the long run, however, the churches suffered from failing to provide for their ministers. J. B. Taylor concluded that "the neglect of ministerial support has been the standing reproach of Virginia Baptists."[10] Thus the families of many ministers suf-

---

[7] Amherst Church in Virginia, formed in 1771, was unique in that it bound itself to pay its minister. Edwards, *op. cit.*, III, 67.

[8] Paschal, *History*, I, 170.

[9] Harvey, *op cit.*, p. 14. James Shelburne, of Halifax County, Virginia, said that he was unwilling to preach "without a pecuniary sacrifice." Taylor, *Virginia Baptist Ministers*, p. 175.

[10] Taylor, *Ibid.*, p. 268.

fered great privation and distress. The churches also suffered a dearth of leadership, when hundreds of ministers moved to frontier regions in order to escape their economic plight.

Early in his ministry, Samuel Harris was most outspoken in his opposition to ministerial support. After some years, however, he visited the home of a traveling pastor, whom he had advised during the preacher's ordination never to take a cent for preaching. He found the family of the minister in dire need. Without delay, Harris confessed to the man's church the error of his earlier view of ministerial support. This acknowledged error brought Harris great remorse. Once he confessed it to a traveling companion with such anguish that he was overcome, and he turned aside into the forest to pour out his confession in prayer.[11] Unhappily, many Separates lacked Harris' views on the evils of nonsupport of the ministry.

Finally, the Separate movement had a weak theology. Simplicity and indefiniteness of theological statement may have fitted the requirements of the frontier, but ultimately this vagueness proved detrimental. Early in the movement two or three doctrines were preached over and over again, which entranced the auditors. Many of the Separate preachers were like William Marshall of whom it was said that "he had not taken time to investigate the mysteries of the Gospel or to prepare to expound the Word of God"[12] before they went forth to preach. Later, men gradually became conscious of the need for a more complete system of thought.

The Separates' aversion to confessions of faith, however, kept them from the pitfall into which the Regulars of eastern North Carolina fell when they elevated a confession to the status of a creed, cherished this creed inordinately, and drifted with it into an unproductive primitivism and quietism.[13] But, on the other hand, the Separates, because of their anticonfessionalism, faced the danger of too much theological variety in the fellowship and took a more consistent theological position.

---
[11] *Ibid.*, pp. 34-35.
[12] *Ibid.*, p. 104.
[13] This was the fate of numbers of churches in the Kehukee Association.

The anticonfessionalism and opposition to ministerial education so often found among the early Separates reappeared on the Kentucky frontier. The South Kentucky Association advertised its stand on both issues. Elsewhere in Kentucky the same Separate views were often expressed. The ground was thus prepared for the Campbellite movement in the 1830's. Alexander Campbell took hold of the popular prejudices against confessions and ministerial education and used them mightily during the early years of his preaching to establish his movement. To the Regular Baptists of the frontier he preached antiorganizationism with great effect, but to the Baptists of Separate background he constantly preached anticonfessionalism and antiministerial education. The result in Kentucky alone was a defection of ten thousand members from Baptist ranks in about ten years.

However, for all its weaknesses, the Separate movement tremendously advanced the cause of religion in America and shaped the character of Protestantism in the South. Mosteller unhesitatingly calls it "the greatest religious movement in America" up to its time.[14] It secured for the Baptists of the South a numerical superiority over other denominations which has never been relinquished. In 1740 there were only six Baptist churches in the region, but by 1790 they numbered 410. Of the 65,233 Baptist church members in the country in 1790, 35,324 of them were to be found in the South, where they had been almost unknown forty years earlier.[15]

Although the general religious influence of the Separate Baptists is worthy of considerable notice, of far greater significance is their specific influence upon the Baptists of the South. It is not too much to say that the Separate Baptists are historically and hereditarily the chief component of Baptist life in the South, both White and Negro.

Although the Regular Baptists preceded the Separates in the South, they were not overactive when the Separates arrived. The

---

[14] Mosteller, *History of Kiokee Church*, p. 36.
[15] Mosteller, "Separate Baptists," p. 153.

Significance of the Movement 155

Regulars had been in the Charleston, South Carolina, area for seventy-five years when Shubal Stearns reached North Carolina, but they had organized only four small churches as late as 1751, when the Charleston Association was formed.

The truth is that throughout America the Regular Baptists had experienced painfully slow growth prior to the Great Awakening, and that when the Awakening came, the Regulars stood aloof. They were wary of its theology, its enthusiasm, and its connections with established churches. The twelve churches connected with the Philadelphia Association, the center of Regular Baptist strength in the colonies in 1740, were not greatly stirred by the Awakening. Hopewell Church in New Jersey was an exception with a great revival ingathering in 1747, 1764, and 1766.

Several men who became outstanding Regular preachers were converted in middle colony revivals of the Awakening. Among them was Benjamin Miller, of Scotch Plains, New Jersey, a convert of Gilbert Tennant. Abel Morgan was inspired by Whitefield's example to preach as an itinerant. Three converts of the Awakening who were to exercise ministries in the South were Oliver Hart, John Gano, and David Thomas. Hart, after hearing Whitefield, was baptized by Jenkin Jones, of Philadelphia, before coming to Charleston, South Carolina, in 1750. Gano, an awakened young Presbyterian, told by one of the Tennants to think for himself on the subject of baptism and not to let the devil destroy his usefulness by indecision, was ordained to the Baptist ministry in 1754. He traveled to South Carolina that same year.[16] Thomas, a convert of Whitefield, came to northern Virginia in 1760 and began a highly effective ministry of evangelization and planting churches. All three of these men had received good educational preparation for the ministry. In respect both to education and revival interest, however, these men were exceptional among the Regular Baptists.

There must have been some stirring of the Philadelphia Association churches in the Awakening, but there was no great en-

---
[16] Maxton, *op. cit.*, pp. 132-33.

thusiasm. In Pennsylvania, Baptists had no notable revival growth. There was growth in New York during the Awakening, but this was due to migration from New England. Only in New Jersey were Regular Baptist churches particularly stirred.

No missionary impulse might have been expected, therefore, from the Philadelphia area, and none was forthcoming. Thomas was sent to Virginia in 1752, and with him went Gano, but the purpose of this visit was to set in order the Ketocton Church at its own request. Then in 1754, in response to an appeal from Hart in Charleston, the Association dispatched Gano to the Regular Baptists of Jersey Settlement, North Carolina. While there, Gano took it upon himself to visit the General Baptists of the region in order to persuade them to Calvinism. Another visit to North Carolina by Gano, Miller and, Van Horn in 1755 apparently was independent of the Association. Thus, it appears that the Regular Baptists were content to accept calls from their own churches or, at most, to convert already existing General Baptist churches. For thirteen years from 1755, the nearest thing to official missionary activity by the Philadelphia Association was the sending of pulpit supplies to affiliated churches.[17] Most representatives sent by the Association gave attention to reorganizing, indoctrinating, or settling difficulties in churches, not evangelizing.

More might have been expected of the Charleston churches, except that they were weak, divided, and unaggressive. Only with the coming of Oliver Hart and Edmund Botsford did they develop a missionary program, but their outreach was not great.

No sharper contrast between churches regarding missionary fervor and outreach can be found than that of the Jersey Regular and the Sandy Creek Separate churches. Located in the same part of North Carolina, they had very different histories. It is true that Indian troubles disturbed the Jersey people in the 1750's, but most of the people continued to live afterward in the same general locality. Jersey never became a mother church, but Sandy Creek was the mother of no less than forty-two churches! The

---

[17] Mosteller, "Separate Baptists," p. 150.

Jersey people drifted apart when their pastor, Gano, left; later they joined other churches, most of them Separate Baptist.

The Regular Baptists, in a word, could never have won the South. They lacked the enthusiasm, the vision, and the leadership required for so formidable an undertaking. To be sure, the Regulars experienced a renewed vigor during the southern Awakening, but this renewal came chiefly from the Separates. The Regulars then made a real contribution to the Awakening, but it was limited in scope. Besides their activities on the Kentucky-Tennessee frontier, they occupied comparatively small areas in northern Virginia and eastern North Carolina and South Carolina. Between 1740 and 1790 they formed only ten churches in Virginia and one in North Carolina, excluding those reorganized from the General Baptists.[18] In the same period, the Separates founded several hundred churches.

In growth the situation was one-sided, but theologically the influence of the Separates was less one-sided. Since they were conscious of their need for a more detailed and systematic theology than the Abbot's Creek summary and because they were sensitive to Regular Baptist accusations of Arminianism among them, they gradually approved an evangelical Calvinistic scheme not far removed from the views of the Virginia Regulars. They would never bind themselves to a strict creed. Neither would they countenance a rigid hyper-Calvinism, such as that of certain Philadelphia Baptist ministers which Backus says denied ministers the right to address all sinners without distinction.[19]

After the Revolution, the Separates tended to strengthen their Calvinistic convictions, although most of them remained moderate Calvinists. Perhaps a statement of John Leland was typical of their position just prior to the union of 1787. He said, "It is a matter of fact that the preaching that has been most blessed of God, and most profitable to men, is the doctrine of sovereign grace in the salvation of souls, mixed with a little of what is called

---
[18] *Ibid.*, p. 153.
[19] *Ibid.*, pp. 146-47.

Arminianism."[20] The challenge of Methodism, and especially of several Baptist ministers influenced by Methodist theology (like Jeremiah Walker and John Waller), served to produce a Calvinistic reaction among most Separates. The reaction was not a severe one, however, and it did not invite Methodist inroads such as were made in Regular Baptist territory in northern Virginia.[21]

Thus, in accommodating the theology of the Regulars, the Separates avoided extreme positions. They subscribed to a moderate Calvinism, which has been fairly normative among Southern Baptists. A primary concern of that theology involves proclaiming the gospel to all men and the obligation of men everywhere to believe it.

In many distinguishable ways the Separate Baptists live on in Southern Baptists. Most notable is the general spirit and outlook of the Southern Baptist people. Much of the aggressiveness and evangelistic outreach of the Separates is repeated in their modern descendants. Thanks to this spirit, and to certain other favorable factors, including a homogeneous old-American community in which to work, freedom, and good organization, Baptists in the South today outnumber those in the North something like five or six to one. Clearly, a paramount explanation of this expansion in the South rests on the foundations laid and the numerical superiority obtained for Baptists in the Separate revival of the eighteenth century. Baptists continue to use techniques of mass evangelism in the South, after the fashion of their Separate forebears. Even when most American Protestant denominations dropped the annual revival meeting during the second quarter of the twentieth century, most Southern Baptist churches continued to use it. Evangelism and missions have ever characterized those churches which stand in the Separate succession.

Certain ecclesiological tendencies of the Separates also persist in

---

[20] Paschal, "Shubal Stearns," p. 54.

[21] In 1813 Benedict reported that although many members of the Sandy Creek Association had once leaned toward the Arminian system, they "have now become generally, and some of them strenuously Calvanistick." Quoted in Mosteller, "Separate Baptists," p. 150.

Baptist life in the South, especially in the Southern Baptist Convention. Although the Separate Baptist movement arose in protest against ecclesiastical centralization and ministerial authority, the Separates themselves soon exhibited tendencies in these directions.

The Separate churches were more closely connected from the beginning than the Regular churches. The Sandy Creek Association was but a few years old when member churches began to complain about the degree of control exercised by the Association over supposedly autonomous churches. The Association divided into three sections over this very matter. To the patriarchal influence of Shubal Stearns, founder of the Separate Baptist movement in the South, has been attributed the high degree of centralization in the Sandy Creek Association. However, this phenomenon appeared repeatedly in succeeding Separate associations, while it almost never appeared among the Regulars.

The Congaree Association, the southern wing of the Sandy Creek Association, experienced the same development. Around 1777, the Association got into trouble, as Morgan Edwards records, by attempting to intrude more in the affairs of the churches than properly belonged to an advisory council. The result was dissolution of the body.

The General Association of Virginia represents a definite reaction against associational authority. At the time of its organization in 1771 this body took special care to ordain that the association never be empowered to impose anything upon the churches, but that it be an advisory council only. There was even some sentiment in Virginia for a polity of complete independence of churches. This radical reaction was curbed, but the decline of the General Association around 1783 must have been due in part to a continuing fear of its usurping local prerogatives. The rapid reaction to the office of apostle among Virginia Baptists points to the same fear. The distinguishing spirit of Virginia Baptists owes an important debt to the eighteenth-century reaction against tendencies of centralization native to the Separate Baptist movement.

On the frontier, the South Kentucky Separate Association exceeded all others in its centralized authority and ministerial elevation. At its first meeting, it decreed that "all ministerial difficulties should be settled by a company of ministers," and that two ministers might suspend or stop any heterodox minister from preaching until the time of his trial.[22] Other Kentucky associations with strong Separate Baptist backgrounds showed these centralizing tendencies.

The Separate Baptist heritage is seen in the type of organizational structure devised for the Southern Baptist Convention in 1844. The Convention was an organizational novelty among Baptists, combining executive features of the associational organization with a few representational features of the society type of organization. Co-operative activities were combined in a denominational pattern. The several boards channeling the resources of the churches in particular directions were all responsible directly to the Convention. Thus the Convention proved a more centralized general unit than Baptists had had anywhere in the world.

The South debated at length the structural pattern for the new convention, but the plan of William B. Johnson of South Carolina prevailed. Johnson favored the efficient unified structure which some had urged vainly at the time of the formation of the Triennial Convention in 1814. The society method of organization had prevailed in this first national Baptist body, but in the South it was decisively rejected in 1845.

Johnson was a disciple of Richard Furman, and from Furman the line back to the Separate Baptists is a direct one. Furman was a convert of Joseph Reese, who was a convert of Philip Mulkey, who was a convert of John Newton, who was a convert of Shubal Stearns. It may be argued that there were also people in the Charleston Regular Association who had gifts for organizing and who were disposed to favor the plan adopted by the Southern Baptist Convention. However, this would only demonstrate an oc-

---

[22] Masters, *op. cit.*, pp. 64, 168.

Significance of the Movement 161

casional agreement of a minority group with the prevailing sentiment of the majority party. Separate Baptists generally showed an instinct for connectionalism at the denominational level, while Regular Baptists habitually shied away from all tendencies to a centralized denomination. The Ketocton Regular Association, for example, was wary of the General Meeting of Correspondence in Virginia as late as 1810 and refused to enter local troubles, even upon invitation.[23] On the other hand, the use of intercongregational presbyteries for ministerial ordination, for organizing churches, and for settling differences within and among congregations was popularized in the South by the Separates.

The Southern Baptist Convention has profited greatly from the efficiency of its organization, but organization may tend to encourage conformity at some expense to local autonomy and freedom.

Other unique features of Separate Baptist practice and outlook have lingered on in Southern Baptist life. The attitudes of self-consciousness and self-sufficiency, of uniqueness and religious detachment, which are sometimes found among Southern Baptists, are not mere provincialisms but are traceable to antecedent attitudes of the Separates. The popular hymnody of Southern Baptists, which stands in marked contrast to the more formal and heavily didactic hymns of the Regulars, is more like the vernacular religious songs of the Separates.

The Southern Baptist insistence on a public profession of faith before the congregation prior to baptism descended from the Separate Baptists, who required vocal and credible testimonies of conversion before the church prior to baptism.

The excellent tradition of lay leadership in church affairs cherished by Southern Baptists owes much to the Separates, who put the affairs of religion for the first time in the South into the hands of laymen.

An unhealthy biblicism appeared from time to time among the Separates, but its deleterious effects did not emerge until after the eighteenth century. The frontier accentuated the conservative,

---
[23] Semple, *op. cit.*, pp. 304, 330.

biblicistic, and separatist tendencies of the Separate Baptist movement. Unique practices were tenaciously retained; the restoration of primitive patterns of church life became a matter of great concern; and divisive movements appeared in the interest of preserving the dissenting character of nonconformist religion.

A new South Kentucky Association of Separate Baptists was formed in 1803 (following the union of 1801) by a small group of churches. It continues to the present as an independent denomination. Another schismatic group, the Original Barren River Association of United Baptists, appeared in 1841. Landmarkism, a far more pervasive movement of high-church views, appeared around 1850. It undoubtedly was motivated by much the same kind of separatist spirit, although a denominational movement apart from the Southern Baptist Convention did not appear until around 1900, when the American Baptist Association was formed in Texas and Arkansas.

However various its fruitage, the Separate Baptist movement contributed notably to the spiritual life and vitality of American Christianity. It infused such life into the Baptist denomination in America as to raise it from obscurity to prominence within a quarter of a century. By reason of this brief history it made Baptists the principal beneficiaries in America of the Great Awakening.

Bibliography

ARMSTRONG, D. W. "An Examination of American Evangelism Beginning with the 18th Century in the Light of N. T. Principles of Evangelism." Unpublished Th.D. dissertation, Southern Baptist Theological Seminary, 1955.

ARNETT, ALEX M. *The Story of North Carolina.* Chapel Hill: University of North Carolina Press, 1933.

BACKUS, ISAAC. *An Abridgement of the Church History of New England from 1620 to 1804.* Boston, 1804.

──────. *A History of New England with Particular Reference to the Denomination of Christians Called Baptists.* Vol. II. Providence, 1784.

BEARDSLEY, F. G. *Religions Progress Through Religious Revivals.* New York: American Tract Society, 1943.

BENEDICT, DAVID. *General History of the Baptist Denomination in America and Other Parts of the World.* Vol. II. New York: Sheldon, Blakeman, & Co., 1856.

BIGGS, JOSEPH. *A Concise History of the Kehukee Baptist Association.* Tarborough, N. C.: George Howard, 1834.

BURRAGE, H. S. *A History of Baptists in New England.* Philadelphia, 1894.

CATHCART, WILLIAM. *The Baptist Encyclopedia.* Vol. II. Philadelphia: Louis H. Everts, 1881.

Congregational Quarterly, The. Boston, 1869. Vol. XI.

CONNOR, R. D. W. *Makers of North Carolina History.* Raleigh: Thompson Publishing Co., 1917.

DENISON, FREDERIC. *Notes of the Baptists, and Their Principles, in Norwich.* Norwich, 1857.

DEVIN, ROBERT I. *A History of Grassy Creek Baptist Church.* Raleigh, 1880.

EDWARDS, MORGAN. "Materials Towards a History of the Baptists in the Provinces of Maryland, Virginia, North Carolina, Georgia." 6 vols. MS in the Furman University Library, Greenville, S. C.

EVANS, PHILIP. *History of Connecticut Baptist State Convention, 1823-1907.* Hartford: Smith-Tinsley Co., 1909.

FRIES, ADELAIDE (ed.). *Records of the Moravians in North Carolina.* Vols. I-VI. Raleigh: State Department of Archives and History of North Carolina, 1943.

GAUSTAD, EDWIN S. "Baptists and the Great Awakening," *The Chronicle*, XV (January, 1952), 41-48.

————. *The Great Awakening in New England.* New York: Harper & Bros., 1957.

GEWEHR, W. M. *The Great Awakening in Virginia, 1740-1790.* Durham, N. C.: Duke University Press, 1930.

GLEDSTONE, J. P. *George Whitfield, M. A. Field Preacher.* London, n.d.

GREENE, L. F. (ed.). *The Writings of the Late Elder John Leland.* New York, 1845.

HARVEY, W. P. *A Sketch of the Life and Times of William Hickman.* Louisville: Baptist World Publishing Co., 1909.

HASSELL, C. B. *History of the Church of God—especially the History of the Kehukee Primitive Baptist Association.* Middletown, N. Y.: Gilbert Beebe's Sons, 1886.

HENRY, STUART C. *George Whitefield, Wayfaring Witness.* Nashville: Abingdon Press, 1957.

History of the Baptist Denomination in Georgia. Compiled for the *Christian Index.* Atlanta: J. P. Harrison & Co., 1881.

HOFFMAN, F. W. *Revival Times in America.* Boston: W. A. Wilde Co., 1956.

HOSKINS, H. P. "Lewis Craig's 'Traveling Church,' " *The Chronicle*, XI (January, 1948), 38-44.

HOWELL, R. B. C. "The Influence of the Baptists on the Formation of the Virginia State Government," *Southern Baptist Review and Eclectic*, II (July and August, 1856), 457-89.

JAMES, CHARLES F. *Documentary History of the Struggle for Religious Liberty in Virginia.* Lynchburg: J. P. Bell Co., 1900.

KELLER, C. R. *The Second Great Awakening in Connecticut.* New Haven: Yale University Press, 1942.

KILPATRICK, J. H. *The Baptists.* Atlanta: Georgia Baptist Convention, 1911.

Life of the Rev. James Ireland. Winchester, Va., 1819.

LITTLE, L. P. *Imprisoned Preachers and Religious Liberty in Virginia.* Lynchburg: J. P. Bell Co., 1938.

MASTERS, FRANK M. *A History of the Baptists in Kentucky.* Louisville: Kentucky Baptist Historical Society, 1953.

MAXTON, C. H. *The Great Awakening in the Middle Colonies.* Chicago: University of Chicago Press, 1920.

McGlothlin, W. J. (ed.). *Publications of the Kentucky Baptist Historical Society.* Louisville: Baptist World Publishing Company, 1910.
Meade, Bishop. *Old Churches, Ministers, and Families of Virginia.* Vol. I. Philadelphia: J. B. Lippincott & Co., 1872.
Meyer, Jacob C. *Church and State in Massachusetts from 1740 to 1833.* Cleveland: Western Reserve University Press, 1930.
Mitchell, M. H. *The Great Awakening and Other Revivals in the Religious Life of Connecticut.* New Haven: Yale University Press, 1934.
Mode, Peter G. *The Frontier Spirit in American Christianity.* New York: Macmillan Co., 1923.
Moore, L. W. *A History of the Middle District Association.* Richmond: Virginia Baptist Historical Society, 1886.
Mosteller, James D. *A History of Kiokee Baptist Church in Georgia.* Ann Arbor: Edwards Bros., Inc., 1952.
—————. "The Separate Baptists in the South," *The Chronicle,* XVII (July, 1954), 143-54.
Newman, A. H. *A History of the Baptist Churches in the United States.* New York: Charles Scribner's Sons, 1915.
Nichols, R. H. "The Influence of the American Environment on the Conception of the Church in American Protestantism," *Church History,* XI (September, 1942), pp. 183-87.
North Carolina Historical Review. Vols. III, VII. Raleigh: North Carolina Historical Society, 1930.
Palmer, Albert G. *A Discourse Delivered at the 100th Anniversary of the Organization of the First Baptist Church in North Stonington, September 20, 1843.* Boston: Gould, Kendall, & Lincoln, 1844.
Paschal, G. W. *History of North Carolina Baptists.* Vol. I. Raleigh: General Board of North Carolina Baptist State Convention, 1930.
—————. *Ibid.,* Vol. II, 1955.
—————. "Shubal Stearns," *Review and Expositor,* XXXVI (January, 1939), 43-57.
Pearce, Stewart. *Annals of Luzerne County.* Philadelphia: J. B. Lippincott & Co., 1960.
Purcell, Richard J. *Connecticut in Transition, 1775-1818.* Washington: American Historical Association, 1918.
Purefoy, G. W. *History of the Sandy Creek Baptist Association.* New York: Sheldon & Co., 1859.
Ragsdale, B. D. *The Story of Georgia Baptists.* Atlanta: Executive Committee, Georgia Baptist Convention, 1938.
Riley, B. F. *Baptists in the Making of the Nation.* Louisville, 1922.

RYLAND, G. H. *History of the Baptists of Virginia*. Richmond: Virginia Baptist Board of Missions and Education, 1955.
SANFORD, E. B. *A History of Connecticut*. Hartford: S. S. Scranton & Co., 1887.
SEAT, W. R. "A History of Tennessee Baptists to 1820-25." Unpublished Th.D. dissertation, Southern Baptist Theological Seminary, 1931.
SEMPLE, A. B. *A History of the Rise and Progress of the Baptists of Virginia*. Revised and extended by G. W. Beale. Richmond: Pitt & Dickinson, 1894.
SHEETS, HENRY. *A History of the Liberty Baptist Association*. Raleigh, 1907.
SWANTON, J. R. *The Indian Tribes of North America*. Smithsonian Institution, Bulletin CXLV. Washington, 1952.
SWEET, W. W. *Revivalism in America*. New York: Charles Scribner's Sons, 1944.
——————. *The Story of Religion in America*. New York: Harper & Bros., 1950.
TAYLOR, J. B. *Virginia Baptist Ministers*. Vol. I. Philadelphia: J. B. Lippincott & Co., 1859.
TAYLOR, JOHN. *History of Ten Churches*. Frankfort, Ky.: J. H. Holeman, 1823.
THOM, W. T. *The Struggle for Religious Freedom in Virginia: The Baptists*. Baltimore: Johns Hopkins Press, 1912.
TOWNSEND, LEAH. *South Carolina Baptists, 1670-1805*. Florence, S. C.: Florence Printing Co., 1935.
TRACY, JOSEPH. *The Great Awakening*. Boston: Tappan & Dennet, 1842.
TYERMAN, L. *The Life of the Rev. George Whitefield*. Vol. I. New York: Randolph & Co., 1877.
WALKER, WILLISTON. *A History of the Congregational Churches in the United States*. New York: Christian Literature Co., 1894.
WILLIAMS, S. C. *The Baptists of Tennessee*. Vol. I. Kingsport: Southern Publishers, Inc., 1930.

www.ingramcontent.com/pod-product-compliance
Lightning Source LLC
Chambersburg PA
CBHW070918180426
43192CB00038B/1755